An honest witness does not deceive,
but a false witness pours out lies.

—Proverbs 14:5 (NIV)

Sweet Carolina MYSTERIES

Roots and Wings
Picture-Perfect Mystery
Angels Watching Over Me
A Change of Art
Conscious Decisions
Surrounded by Mercy
Broken Bonds
Mercy's Healing
To Heal a Heart
A Cross to Bear
Merciful Secrecy
Sunken Hopes
Hair Today, Gone Tomorrow
Pain Relief
Redeemed by Mercy
A Genius Solution

Sweet Carolina MYSTERIES

A GENIUS SOLUTION

DeAnna Julie Dodson

Sweet Carolina Mysteries is a trademark of Guideposts.

Published by Guideposts
100 Reserve Road, Suite E200
Danbury, CT 06810
Guideposts.org

Copyright © 2023 by Guideposts. All rights reserved.

This book, or parts thereof, may not be reproduced, stored in a retrieval system, or transmitted in any form or by any means, electronic, mechanical, photocopying, recording, or otherwise, without the written permission of the publisher.

This is a work of fiction. While the setting of Mercy Hospital as presented in this series is fictional, the location of Charleston, South Carolina, actually exists, and some places and characters may be based on actual places and people whose identities have been used with permission or fictionalized to protect their privacy. Apart from the actual people, events, and locales that figure into the fiction narrative, all other names, characters, businesses, and events are the creation of the author's imagination and any resemblance to actual persons or events is coincidental.

Every attempt has been made to credit the sources of copyrighted material used in this book. If any such acknowledgment has been inadvertently omitted or miscredited, receipt of such information would be appreciated.

Scripture references are from the following sources: *The Holy Bible, King James Version* (KJV). *The Holy Bible, New International Version* (NIV). Copyright © 1973, 1978, 1984, 2011 by Biblica, Inc. Used by permission of Zondervan. All rights reserved worldwide. www.zondervan.com.

Cover and interior design by Müllerhaus
Cover illustration by Bob Kayganich at Illustration Online LLC.
Typeset by Aptara, Inc.

This book was previously published under the title *A Genius Solution* as part of the *Miracles & Mysteries of Mercy Hospital* series.

ISBN 978-1-959634-73-7 (hardcover)
ISBN 978-1-959634-75-1 (epub)

Printed and bound in the United States of America
10 9 8 7 6 5 4 3 2 1

A GENIUS SOLUTION

Chapter One

"WHAT DO YOU THINK?" JOY ATKINS leaned closer to her friends as they sat drinking coffee around the little table in the back of the Mercy Hospital gift shop Wednesday afternoon. "But really, it ought to be a surprise."

Evelyn Perry took the pencil from the knot of silver hair at the nape of her neck and immediately started taking notes. "It's the twentieth, right?"

Joy nodded. "This coming Tuesday. And yes, I know we're cutting it close already."

"All right, we'd better get busy then." Evelyn jotted down the date. "Who did you think of inviting?"

"I hadn't actually gotten that far yet," Joy admitted. "I was only wondering what you two thought of the idea."

"I like it," Anne Mabry said, her blue eyes warm. "Shirley's been so busy lately that she probably hasn't even had time to think about her birthday yet."

The three of them, along with Mercy nurse Shirley Bashore, were close friends, and a birthday in the group was always reason to celebrate. Though the women were of varying ages, marital statuses, and ethnic backgrounds, their friendship was rock solid. It was a testament to the two important traits they had in common: a dedication to helping people in need and a strong faith in God.

Joy smiled. "I'm sure Garrison has something wonderful in the works for her." The much-respected Mercy hospital administrator, Garrison Baker, was also tall, dark, and handsome. He and Shirley had been dating the last few months and things looked like they could be getting serious.

"We can always have it before the day, if we need to. Ralph and I would be happy to help however we can."

"I appreciate it, but I know you both have a lot going on with Lili going to school. Addie still needs you."

Ralph was Anne's husband, the hospital chaplain, and Addie was the eight-year-old granddaughter they had been raising while their daughter, Lili, was in the military. Lili was back home now and Addie was living with her again, but Ralph and Anne were still very involved in their lives.

Anne sighed. "It's always something. But Ralph and I are glad to help when Lili is busy." She patted Joy's arm. "That doesn't mean we can't help you too."

"I don't think it's going to be a big deal," Joy assured her. "Just some friends. I thought we could go to a nice restaurant and have dinner."

"Which one did you have in mind?" Evelyn asked, and she wrote *Restaurant?* on her pad of paper.

"I remember how much Shirley enjoyed going to Revival with Garrison a while ago. She hasn't stopped talking about how good the seafood was. What do you two think?"

"She's mentioned it to me a couple of times," Anne said. "But I wasn't sure if she enjoyed it so much because of the food or because she was out with Garrison."

"So just the seven of us?" Joy asked.

"What about Roger?" Evelyn held her pencil poised to write his name.

"I'll mention it to him," Joy said, feeling a touch of warmth in her face.

She and Roger Gaylord, one of the hospital's major donors, had gone out casually a few times since last Christmas, but Joy wouldn't have minded seeing him more.

"Excellent," Anne said.

"Okay then," Joy said. "You two make sure your husbands are available Tuesday night. I'll talk to Roger and Garrison. I'm thinking we can imply it's only going to be the four of us, and then she'll be surprised to see the guys there too."

"Do you want me to make the reservation?" Evelyn asked.

"I'll take care of it," Joy said. "Anything else we want to consider? Gifts?"

"Definitely." Evelyn stirred more creamer into her coffee. "I know exactly what I want to get for her."

"Yes, definitely gifts," Anne said.

They discussed what Shirley might like for her birthday, and Evelyn wrote everything down.

"Okay." Joy got up and tucked Evelyn's list into her purse. "I'll take care of everything. You two just plan to get your husbands there on time. I'll tell Shirley I'll pick her up at her house because the location is a surprise too, okay?"

Anne nodded eagerly. "That ought to be—"

She broke off when a teenage girl, blond and tan, came into the shop.

"I'll be right with you, Daisy," Joy said.

"Oh, no hurry," Daisy replied, looking over the selection of candies at the front counter, but there was something in her low voice that made Joy study her a little more closely. She looked as if she had recently been crying.

Anne and Evelyn raised their eyebrows at Joy, and she gave them a subtle shake of her head.

"I'd better take care of business," she said. "I think I've got enough information to go from here, don't you think?"

"I'd better get back to the work," Evelyn said, swallowing another quick drink of her coffee. "I've stretched my afternoon break about as far as it will go. Those records aren't going to file themselves."

"I'll talk to Ralph," Anne added, and both of them hurried out of the shop.

Joy immediately went to Daisy. "What can I do for you?"

Daisy swallowed hard and managed a slight smile. "Mr. Bell in 231 wants some licorice, red and definitely not black. I don't see any."

Daisy Graham was a high school senior who volunteered at the hospital several afternoons a week. She was usually cheerful and outgoing, but something was obviously bothering her today.

"I'm sorry," Joy said sympathetically. "We don't usually stock licorice. Maybe we ought to. Is there anything else Mr. Bell would like?"

"He said jelly beans, if you don't have licorice. But not the black ones."

"We have jelly beans." Joy picked up a box. "But they're all colors. There are some black ones in there. Do you think he can eat around those?"

"Sure." Daisy gave her a five-dollar bill. "He said to take it out of that."

Joy rang up the sale and then gave her the candy, the change, and the receipt.

"Thanks," Daisy said, and she turned to leave.

"Daisy?"

Joy couldn't let her go when she was so obviously upset. She didn't know the girl well, but she seemed so helpful and sweet, Joy couldn't help wanting to comfort her.

Daisy turned, her eyebrows raised.

"Would you like some coffee?"

The girl looked wistfully toward the table in the back room. "Mr. Bell will be wondering where I am."

"Do you think he'll mind? Or you could run them up to him and come back. What do you think?"

This time her smile reached her eyes. "I'll be back."

By the time Joy had poured a cup of coffee for Daisy and a fresh one for herself, the high schooler was back.

"I was afraid I was going to see Mrs. Sherman again," she said, glancing behind her as if she was being followed. "I'm not quite ready for that."

"Come sit down," Joy said, leading the way to the table, glad Daisy's usual good spirits had for the most part returned. "Tell me what happened. Who's Mrs. Sherman?"

Daisy blew out a breath, making her blond bangs flutter. "Mrs. Sherman is Connor's mother. Connor goes to my school. He's fifteen, well, he'll be sixteen pretty soon, but he's already a senior."

"Wait a minute. Is his mother's name Veronica?"

Daisy took the coffee Joy offered her and added a generous amount of sugar. "How did you know?"

"She lives down the street from me. She has a daughter too, doesn't she?"

"Yeah, Hailey. She's away at college though."

"Right. I think I heard that. But what is Veronica doing here? She's not sick, is she?"

"No," Daisy said. "It's Connor. He's here because he hurt his knee and had to have surgery."

"Oh. I heard he has some health problems too. I hope the injury isn't serious."

"It's not great, but he ought to recover okay. He's been doing really well lately otherwise. He thinks he's grown out of a lot of the problems he had before, really bad asthma and that kind of thing. He wants to start applying to the colleges he's interested in, but his mom won't let him until she's sure he's doing all right physically."

"I'm glad it's nothing too serious then," Joy said. "But isn't he a little young to be applying to colleges yet? He's a senior already?"

"Yeah, he's been in my class the past three years. He probably could have moved up another year pretty easy, but his mother didn't think it was good for him. Socially, I mean. He says he's pretty bored, but he does a lot of reading on his own. He's really interested in thermodynamics."

Joy chuckled. "I don't think I'm even sure what that is much less how it works."

Daisy rolled her eyes. "Just ask him, and he'll tell you all about it."

"You're not friends?"

"He's only a kid, you know? I mean, he ought to be hanging out with the freshmen or sophomores or something, not with the seniors. Besides, there's only one Lackland Scholarship, and that's for the class valedictorian."

"The Lackland Scholarship?"

"Yeah. I've been aiming toward it since I was a freshman. A guy named James Lackland was valedictorian at our school years ago. He got rich in electronics, and he set up a scholarship for whoever ended up being the class valedictorian every year. It's a pretty impressive amount, and it would let whoever gets it pay for just about any college in the country."

"That's a great incentive," Joy said.

"It really is. People my age shouldn't have to compete for it against kids his age."

"I see."

Daisy shrugged. "Connor's all right, I guess. In a lot of ways he's had it kind of hard, being sick as often as he was and people always picking on him for being a brainiac and everything. And a mama's boy."

"Is he?"

"Oh, I don't know. She wants him to be, but I think he's getting pretty tired of it. Between her and the lady making a film about him and the doctor who's doing some kind of study on him, he's got to feel pretty fed up by now."

"Probably," Joy said gently, "but what happened with his mother? Did she say something to you?"

Daisy looked into her barely tasted coffee. "I was only trying to be helpful."

Joy waited a moment, but Daisy didn't elaborate.

"What happened?" Joy asked finally.

"I was in the waiting room up on the second floor. Ms. Kingston always says that if we volunteers don't have anything to do, we ought to make sure the waiting rooms are tidy. Anyway, I was in there, and I picked up some newspapers somebody had left in one of the chairs and on the floor. I took them to the trash can, and I noticed an unopened envelope that had the logo of one of the colleges I had applied to. I thought that was kind of strange, so I picked it up, and I saw that it was addressed to Connor Sherman."

"Do you think he could have thrown it away in there?"

"I guess he could have, but I don't know why. His mother usually brings him his mail from home, and then, if there's something he doesn't want, he throws it away in the trash in his room. And she doesn't like him leaving the room if she's not with him."

No wonder the boy was ready for a little independence.

"Besides," Daisy said, "the envelope wasn't open, so I don't know why he would have thrown it away. And it was partly covered up by some of the napkins from the coffee station, but I guess those were thrown in there after the letter."

"Maybe," Joy said thoughtfully. "But what happened with Connor's mother? What did she say to you?"

Daisy looked down again. "I took the letter back to Connor's room. I mean, it was the right thing to do, wasn't it? If he didn't want it, he could just throw it away again, right?"

"You'd think so."

"I gave it to Connor, and he asked me where I found it. I told him, and his mother got really mad at me. She said I must have taken it when Connor was out of the room having tests. She said she brought the mail and, because he wasn't there, she went to the coffee shop for a few minutes. She hadn't even noticed that the letter was missing, because the rest of the mail was sitting there on the table where she'd left it."

"But if you did steal it, why would you have brought it back?"

"That's what *I* said!" Frustrated tears welled up in Daisy's eyes. "She told me I must have realized that stealing mail was a federal offense. She said it was a good thing I brought it back before the police came to get me."

"Oh, honey." Joy reached across the table and squeezed Daisy's hand. "I'm sorry. That must have been very upsetting for you."

"I didn't take that stupid letter." Daisy grabbed a napkin and blotted her face. "I wouldn't."

"You have to remember that Mrs. Sherman is dealing with a lot right now. Having her son in the hospital, even if it's only for tests, has to be hard. And I can imagine having him want to go away to college soon has to be hard on her too. He's still very young."

"I know."

"What did you tell her?"

"I didn't get a chance to explain. That lady who's been filming Connor came in, and I thought I'd better leave." Daisy took a deep breath. "I guess I'm going to have to go back up there and try to explain. Do you think I ought to apologize?"

"It doesn't sound like you did anything wrong, but clearing the air is probably a good idea."

Joy wanted to go with her, but wasn't sure that was a good idea. Daisy was a young woman, and she needed to know she could deal with these things on her own.

"I've always found that the sooner I deal with something, the easier it is to get past."

Daisy nodded gloomily. "That's what my dad always says. And he says I have to do things myself too, if I'm ever going to grow up."

Joy gave her a warm smile. "Smart man."

"Okay." Daisy took a moment to finish her coffee. "I guess I'll go now."

Joy walked her to the door. "The best thing to do is not make a big deal of it, all right? Just tell her you want a chance to explain, and tell her what happened. You don't have anything to apologize for, but if you want to be extra nice, you can tell her you're sorry she was upset."

Daisy laughed softly. "All right. I might do that too. Thanks for letting me talk to you."

"You're always welcome. Any time. Now, go and get it over with, and then have a great rest of your day."

"I will," Daisy assured her.

Joy watched her head toward the lobby and then said a little prayer that Veronica Sherman would at least hear her out.

Joy didn't see Daisy again that day, but when she was ready to go home, she decided to go upstairs and pay the Shermans a visit. She found Connor there alone, reclining in his bed as he read a book evidently about quantum field theory, whatever that was, and there was a wooden puzzle cube on the table beside him. He was tall and thin and pale, and his right knee was elevated and bandaged, resting in a brace.

She knocked on the open door. "May I come in?"

"Sure," he said, his hazel eyes uncertain under his dark brows. He obviously didn't recognize her.

"You might not remember me, but we're neighbors," she told him. "I'm Joy Atkins. I live in the little blue house a couple of doors down from you."

A sudden smile animated his face. "Oh yeah, I remember seeing you now. You came by to check if our WiFi was out that one time."

"That was me." She touched the back of the chair next to his bed. "Mind if I sit down a minute?"

He shrugged. "Please. Mom ought to be back soon."

Joy sat down. "Actually, I came to see how you were. I work in the gift shop downstairs, and I heard you were in the hospital, so I thought I'd come say hi."

"Thanks," he said, a touch of color in his pale cheeks. "Um, how did you know I was here?"

"Daisy Graham is one of our volunteers. She told me."

The color in his face intensified. "That must have been after Mom snapped at her. She looked pretty upset."

"I think she only meant to be helpful," Joy said diplomatically. "Daisy would never—"

"I'm glad you're here. I was planning to get in touch with you about your daughter when I got home this evening."

Joy turned to see a dark-haired woman standing in the doorway. It was Veronica Sherman, Connor's mother.

Chapter Two

STARTLED, JOY STOOD UP AND gave Connor's mother what she hoped was a disarming smile.

"You might not remember me, Mrs. Sherman, but I'm Joy Atkins. I live down the street from you. We met a few months ago when the road construction crew accidentally knocked out the internet service in our area."

Veronica Sherman glanced at her son, who was looking highly embarrassed as he lay back against his pillows, the book he'd been reading clutched in one hand.

She blinked her wide-set hazel eyes at Joy and then fluttered her hands in the air. "Oh dear. I'm so sorry. I do remember you now. It's been a difficult day, and I don't seem to know if I'm coming or going."

"That's all right. I was telling Connor that I heard he was here at the hospital, and I thought it would be neighborly of me to come see how he's doing. I work at the gift shop."

"That was very nice of you." Connor's mother pulled up the chair that was in the corner of the room. "Please sit down again. You know, as many times as I've been in the hospital with Connor, it can get to be a little bit tedious. Not that I wouldn't do anything in the world for him, of course, but it's nice to have a little adult conversation from time to time too."

Connor gazed down at the cover of his book, his lips pressed into a hard line.

"I'm sure it is," Joy said, her tone light as she sat once more.

"But I heard you talking about Daisy Graham, and I assumed you must be her mother. I see she must have told you what happened earlier."

Joy nodded.

"I realize that I overreacted, and I said as much when she came back up a little while later, but really, what was I supposed to think?"

"She told me she tried to explain what happened."

"She did, but Swarna came up just then and brought that puzzle, and I knew she wanted to talk to Connor, and I didn't really have time to deal with a distraction like that. I just let everything get to me. I still don't know how that letter could have gotten into the waiting room, much less into the trash. I thought it was still with the rest of the mail I brought up this morning."

"But I think Daisy has a point. Why would she bring it back if she was the one who took it in the first place?"

"I couldn't think of anything but that she was afraid she'd get in trouble for taking it and thought she'd better bring it back. Who else but someone competing for the same scholarships as Connor would be interested in it?"

"It was only an invitation to talk to some people on campus, Mom," Connor said. "It's not like it was an actual offer or anything. And it had nothing to do with the scholarship the school is offering."

"I know. I know. But there are other scholarships out there, and I can't figure out who else would have taken it."

"I got it back," he said reasonably. "Isn't that what matters?"

"Yes." Suddenly her worry seemed to lift. "It's not as if that school wouldn't have gotten in touch with you again if they didn't hear back from you. Everybody wants you as a student."

"Not everybody," Connor said, and Joy was surprised he managed not to squirm.

"Mrs. Sherman," she began.

"Oh, call me Veronica, please."

"All right, Veronica, if you'll call me Joy."

"I will." Veronica seemed genuinely grateful. "And I truly am sorry I snapped at the girl. She didn't deserve that, even if she had done something wrong."

"Mom," Connor reproved.

"Okay, I'm not saying I know she did."

"And not everybody's out to get me," he added.

"All right. All right."

"Daisy said she was sorry Mom got upset," Connor told Joy. "I thought that was nice of her."

"I think so too," Joy told him.

"She told me she understood about the stress I've been under," Veronica said. "And I always get a little bit nervous when Swarna comes around. I mean, she's very sweet and I really appreciate her, but she's very direct and always in a hurry. And she talks too fast. I mean, I used to be a nurse before my boy came along and needed so much looking after, so I'm not unused to a demanding pace, but she is always on the go. She's a very important person, a real artist. It's amazing just to know her."

"You mentioned Swarna before. Who's that?"

"Oh my goodness," Veronica said, lighting up. "If you haven't heard of Swarna LeFrye, you will before too much longer. She's a filmmaker. All kinds of arty, experimental sorts of things mostly. She's won so many awards."

"From places nobody's ever heard of," Connor said under his breath.

"She has to start somewhere, doesn't she? And her work is very good."

"What kind of films does she do?" Joy asked.

"Most of them are very intellectual. Very deep. Like she had one that followed this willow branch down a stream. At first it was very slow and idyllic and the camera work was really lovely, all that dappled sunlight through the trees playing off the water. Then lots of things got in its way, but in spite of everything, it still kept moving along. Finally it came to a waterfall and was swept violently away. Oh." Veronica put both hands over her heart. "I know that's not a very good summary of the film, but it was very moving. Heartbreaking, really."

Connor rolled his eyes.

His mother gave him a reproving look. "Anyway, they're all very different from each other, I'm given to understand. I haven't watched the ones that are supposed to be very gritty, but she's done some on the inner cities and in some of the poorer parts of Africa and the Middle East that have been groundbreaking. She did a whole series on French street mimes and what their lives are really like."

"She's certainly covered a wide range of subjects," Joy observed. "What does that have to do with Connor? Is he one of her subjects?"

"He's the main one," Veronica said with undisguised pride. "She's been filming him since he wasn't even two years old."

"Really?"

"Oh yes. In fact, she was filming when he hurt his knee."

Connor gave Joy a sheepish grin. "I tripped over her camera bag. I thought it was out of the way."

"You shouldn't have been playing so hard," Veronica told him. "Especially with those rowdy Miller boys."

"Mom," Connor protested. "We were having fun. They're all right."

"Well, the last thing you needed was knee surgery."

Connor sighed.

"Anyway," Veronica told Joy, "Swarna's been following Connor for years. He was such a smart baby, we had to have him tested, and then Dr. Dahlman started studying him. Swarna was talking to him about some of his very young patients, wanting to find one she could follow at least through his school years. She was interested in showing the effects that high intelligence has on children's socialization. They thought Connor would be the perfect subject."

"Lab rat," Connor muttered.

"You must have been pretty smart," Joy told him.

He shrugged.

"Well, you were." Veronica turned to Joy. "When he was a baby, we had a big painting of horses over our fireplace. Like we did with everything, we'd tell him what they were. We'd tell him 'horse' or 'horses.' He'd reach toward the picture and say 'agsin.' No matter how many times we told him those were horses, he'd say 'agsin.' We couldn't figure it out, until his father pointed out that the artist had signed his name in bold letters at the bottom of the canvas. It was Jackson."

If there was any truth to the story, it was pretty amazing.

"Do you remember that?" Joy asked Connor. "Do you remember learning to read?"

He shrugged. "Not at all. I just always could."

"Your mom or dad never taught you?"

"Not that I remember."

Joy looked at Veronica.

"We never did," she said. "We had a hard time with his big sister, Hailey. She would never sit still long enough to look at a book, but thank goodness, she's at Clemson now, majoring in ancient languages. Jamie would be so proud of both of them."

"Jamie?"

"Jamie was my husband. He passed away when Connor was twelve and Hailey was fifteen."

"I'm sorry. That must have been very hard on all of you."

"He left us very well provided for," Veronica said with a tight smile. "But that can never make up for not having him with us."

"Of course not. It's a difficult age for them to have lost their father, but I don't think anybody is ever really ready for that, no matter when it happens. You seem to have done a fine job on your own."

Veronica shrugged modestly. "It's my job to prepare them to take on the world, isn't it? Still…"

She glanced at Connor, and Joy could tell she wasn't as ready to let go as she claimed. She knew when her youngest was gone, she'd really be on her own.

She looked appealingly at Joy. "I really am sorry about what I said to Daisy. I could have handled the situation so much better. I'm supposed to be the adult in the room, aren't I?"

"I don't think you should worry about it anymore," Joy said. "I'm sure Daisy understands what you've been dealing with, and it sounds like you worked things out with her. I'm glad. Mostly though, I wanted to see how Connor was doing and to let you know I'm just downstairs or down the street if I can do anything to help."

"That's so nice of you. Sometimes I feel like I'm totally isolated, but then I realize that I only have to reach out."

"I know what you mean," Joy said. "I'm a widow too. I lived in Texas until my husband died and then moved here a little while afterward."

"Oh my. That was a big step to take."

"True, but my daughter and her family are here in Charleston, so it's been nice being closer to them. And, of course, I have my hospital family. I don't know what I'd do without them."

"This must be a lovely place to work," Veronica said. "Everyone here is always so nice. The hospital I worked for back in LA was much more, I don't know, businesslike isn't quite the word, because Mercy is very well run. I suppose it was more impersonal or something."

"We have a wonderful staff." Joy couldn't help beaming at her. "What do you think, Connor?"

Connor looked thoroughly bored, but he was polite enough to have not gone back to his book. "Everybody's been great. They always are. One of them even went and bought me a new bookmark when I misplaced the one I was using. But I'm hoping I won't have to be back here again for a long, long time."

"That depends on what the doctor says," his mother reminded him. "You've been doing really well lately, but we want to make sure there's nothing we need to be looking out for."

"I know, Mom."

"He's not sick right now," Veronica told Joy. "His asthma hasn't come back or anything. Dr. Dahlman is doing a few tests while he's here, but he should be going home as soon as his knee is up to it."

"I'm glad."

"Oh, so are we."

"Who's your doctor?" Joy asked Connor.

"Dr. Morton. He's been taking care of me since I was a kid."

"He's very good, and he's a nice man too."

"Yes," Veronica said uncertainly. "He and Dr. Dahlman don't always agree, but I suppose they work things out eventually."

"I don't believe I know a Dr. Dahlman."

"He's not actually affiliated with the hospital. He's in private practice, mostly research now. He's been taking care of Connor for a long time."

"You mean he's been studying me," Connor said.

"You don't like Dr. Dahlman?" Joy asked.

"Oh, he's fine. He's not creepy or anything. But he sure asks a lot of questions. The same ones a lot of times too. It drives me crazy."

"What exactly is he studying?"

"He takes a lot of scans of my brain and compares them to the ones he took before. And then he asks me a lot about what I'm reading and if school is interesting for me and what I'm planning to do in the future. And I have to do a lot of cognitive and logistical trials. And now he's even happier because he can study the effect of my pain meds on my cognitive function. He says he wants to document 'changes in the genius brain from childhood to maturity.'"

Joy smiled to hear him use a gruff, professional tone for that last part.

He sighed. "I don't know if I can hack this until I'm eighteen."

"Now, he's been very good to you," Veronica said. "Besides taking care of all the study expenses, he's set up a trust to help you with college too."

"Yeah, that's nice of him, but Dad left enough for that, didn't he?"

"Of course he did, but I'd think you'd be flattered to know that, out of all the kids he could have chosen, Dr. Dahlman picked you."

"He's a good guy. I know. I know. Can't I just be normal for a few minutes?"

Joy thought this must not have been the first time mother and son had had this conversation. She stood up with a smile.

"I'm sure whatever information he can get from this study will be very helpful to doctors in the future. Anyway, I've got to head for home now. I mean it though. If either of you need anything, you know where to find me."

"Thanks, Mrs. Atkins."

"You're welcome. And you can call me Joy too."

He grinned.

"Thank you, Joy," Veronica said.

"We're neighbors," Joy told her. "Isn't that what neighbors do? I'm sorry I haven't taken the time to get to know more of mine."

"It's my fault too. Taking care of everything Connor's involved in and getting Hailey into college have taken up every spare minute for the past couple of years. It's nice to know you'll be around when we're here."

"I get here early most mornings," Joy said, "and I generally leave at three. That gives me a lot of time for what I need to do at home."

Veronica stood up too. "Thank you for coming to visit. Maybe we could have lunch or something sometime soon."

"I'd like that. I'll see you both soon."

Joy walked into the corridor and headed toward the elevator, her thoughts turning again to the plans for Shirley's birthday dinner. She decided she really ought to talk to Garrison first before making any other decisions. He might have already asked Shirley out for that evening.

Before Joy could even press the button, the elevator dinged, the double doors opened, and Garrison Baker stepped out.

Chapter Three

"Hey, Joy. How are you?" Garrison asked, his deep brown eyes warming. "I was planning to come talk to you before you left for the day, and I let the time get away from me." He held the elevator doors open. "Do you have a minute now? Or am I keeping you from something?"

"Go ahead and let it go," Joy said. "I was actually going to see if I could ask a favor of you, so it looks like we're both in luck."

He stepped away from the doors, and they shut behind him, the floor lights indicating its rapid descent.

"How about the waiting room?" he suggested. "We could sit for a minute and talk, if you like."

"That would be great."

Joy followed him down the hallway, smiling to herself as she thought what a nice match he and Shirley would make someday. Yes, he could be unwaveringly businesslike, even gruff at times, but clearly Shirley had seen something in him that made her want to develop a friendship, maybe more as things went along. He was a nice-looking man too, his dark skin relatively unlined and his graying hair in a low-cut, almost-military style.

He opened the waiting room door and let her go in first. She was glad, at least for now, that they had found it empty. They sat down in front of the window that overlooked the harbor and the wide, rolling sea beyond.

"Now," he said, "what can I do for you?"

"I didn't know if you were aware, but Shirley's birthday is on the twentieth. Tuesday."

He patted a little notebook that was in his shirt pocket and smiled. "I did know that. I made sure to put it in my iPhone."

"I'm surprised Shirley mentioned it to you."

"She did, as a matter of fact, but it was back in January. I forget why, but I decided I'd take note so I'd remember when it came around in the fall."

"Well, that's exactly why I wanted to talk to you. I was wondering if you had already made plans for that evening. Or if you were planning to ask Shirley to go out with you."

"I did say something to her about it, nothing heavy or anything. I only asked her if she had anything planned, and she said she hadn't even thought about it yet."

"That sounds like Shirley."

Garrison nodded, one side of his mouth turned up. "Anyway, there's a jazz concert this Saturday, so I thought we'd take that in and have a little dinner too. I was going to ask you what her favorite place is."

"She really liked it when you took her to Revival, but I'm not sure whether that was because of the food or the company."

He laughed low. "I think she did enjoy it, but I hate to repeat myself. Do you think she likes Italian? There's a great little place, a mom-and-pop hole-in-the-wall that makes the best chicken parmesan I ever had. And their cream of potato soup is amazing."

"I'm sure she'd love it."

"Just don't say anything to her, all right?"

"I'll keep your secret if you'll keep mine," Joy told him.

"All right. What's yours?"

"Actually, I was talking to Anne and Evelyn this morning about what we could do for Shirley's birthday, and we thought it would be fun if we asked her to have dinner with the three of us at Revival." Joy couldn't help a slight grin. "So I'm glad you decided against going to that particular place."

"That sounds nice, but I'm not sure how I come into it."

Joy realized she should cut to the chase. "Well, what would make it special is when we got to the restaurant, you and James and Ralph and whoever I invite would be waiting for us. What do you think?"

"I think she'd enjoy that, and I'd love to be there with her."

"Wonderful. Consider yourself invited. I don't have the actual details yet as far as the time. I have to coordinate it with everyone, and I have to see if the person I have in mind is interested in coming too."

"I'm certain you'll get it all worked out. You let me know, and I'll make sure to be there."

"Great. And mum's the word, right?"

"For you too," he said, pretending to be stern. "I haven't talked to Shirley yet about that concert." He stood up. "For now, I'd better get going. One of my neighbors is on this floor, and I promised I'd go see how he's doing."

"I'd better get busy too," she said. "I'll let you know the plan when I have one."

"All right then. I'll talk to you soon."

At the doorway of the waiting room, he turned to go down the hall and she went back to the elevator. She caught a startled breath when this time the doors opened and Shirley herself stepped out, her natural bronze skin tone looking resplendent against her gold-colored scrubs. Fortunately, Garrison was already out of sight.

"Isn't this kind of late for you?" she asked Joy, a smile bringing out the dimples in her cheeks.

"It's not that late. I found out one of my neighbors has a son in the hospital, so I thought I'd say hello before I went home. What are you up to?"

Shirley pushed back a strand of curly, silver-streaked dark hair that had escaped the ponytail at the nape of her neck. "The usual this and that."

"I have a question for you though," Joy said.

"Fire away."

"Anne, Evelyn, and I were talking earlier, and we were wondering what you were thinking of doing for your birthday."

"I'm planning to be older and better than ever."

Joy smiled at her enthusiasm. "Are you going to be busy that night? We thought maybe Garrison had asked you out."

She shrugged, seeming unsure. "It'll probably be Mama and me on our own. Maybe I'll get some takeout."

"What if you had a nice dinner with me, Anne, and Evelyn? If you don't have anything else going on, we thought we'd kidnap you and take you out somewhere fancy. What do you think?"

"That would be fun, but I don't want y'all to go to any trouble."

"We like to have fun too, you know, and you had to guess we'd want to do something for you, right? Our little group wouldn't be the same without you."

"I don't usually do that much for my birthday, but it would be nice."

"And if Garrison ends up asking you out that night," Joy said, glad she already knew that wasn't going to happen, "just let us know, and we'll arrange it for a different day. How would that be?"

"I'm sure he and I will do something, but we don't have actual plans yet, so let's go ahead and plan for the four of us to go out on Tuesday."

Joy kept her expression neutral, not wanting to give away any secrets for Saturday. "All right. I'll let Anne and Evelyn know we're on and make the reservations for us. Maybe I can reserve a private dining room in case you get out of hand."

Shirley snickered. "You never can tell when I might cut loose." She squeezed Joy's arm. "Thanks for thinking of me. That was nice of y'all."

"We're always up for a party."

Shirley looked at her slyly. "And you're not going to tell me where we're going?"

"Nope."

"Not even a little hint?"

"Okay," Joy said reluctantly, "it's a place in North America."

"Great," Shirley deadpanned. "Thanks a lot."

"You'll find out on your birthday, so leave it at that. Wear something casually dressy, something comfortable, and that's all you have to do. We'll take care of everything else."

"I'll make sure Mama has somebody to stay with her during the evening."

Joy started to ask her if they ought to invite her mother, Regina, and then she stopped herself. She'd ask Anne and Evelyn what they thought before she said anything. Maybe Shirley would like to have a special evening just with her mother.

"I'll let you know details as soon as I have them," Joy said. "This is going to be fun."

"I think so too," Shirley admitted. "I think we'll have a great time."

"We'll do our best. Anyway, I'd better go see if I can catch Anne while she's still here and then talk to Evelyn. Now we can make some real plans."

"Okay. I'll see you soon."

Shirley turned toward the patients' rooms, and Joy rang for the elevator again. When it arrived this time, it was empty.

She went straight to the chaplain's office, but Anne wasn't there.

"I'm sorry, you just missed her," her husband, Ralph, said, his eyes kind behind his glasses. "She went to pick up Addie from school, and then they were going to buy her a new pair of shoes. The ones she got last week evidently don't fit her right."

"Okay. Thanks."

"You can always get her on her cell phone if it's important."

"No, it sounds like she and Addie are on a mission. I'll talk to her later. Did she happen to tell you about Shirley's birthday?"

"She did," Ralph said. "I'll make sure to keep my calendar open."

"I chatted with Shirley a few minutes ago, and she's available that night, so we're good to go. I'll text Anne with the details."

"Great."

"Thanks, Ralph. I'll see you."

Joy walked over to the records department, wanting to tell Evelyn they were good to go on Tuesday, but she stopped before she opened the door. She could hear low, intense voices on the other side. It wasn't arguing, but evidently something urgent was going on. One of those voices was Evelyn's. She very likely wouldn't have time for anything as frivolous as planning for a birthday dinner. Joy would text her too.

Joy walked away from the records department, through the hospital lobby, and toward the door. There wasn't that much to be done anyway. Garrison was taken care of, she'd talked to Shirley to confirm she was free on Tuesday, and Anne and Evelyn could see that their husbands were on board. All Joy had to do was make the reservations and find an appropriate gift. That was something she could discuss with Anne and Evelyn later on too.

She reached the front door as Veronica Sherman came in. She was in the company of a portly man with black brows, thick glasses, salt-and-pepper hair, and a full beard. He looked as if he was in his late fifties, though a beard often made a man look much older than he actually was.

"Oh, hello, Joy," Veronica said, her eyes alight. "It's funny we should run into you. I was just telling Dr. Dahlman what a surprise it was to have one of my neighbors working here and how nice you were to come see Connor earlier." She glanced at him and then seemed to remember herself. "I'm sorry, Joy. This is Dr. Dahlman, the specialist I was telling you about. The one who's been studying Connor practically his whole life. Dr. Dahlman, this is Joy Atkins. She lives right down the street from me."

"It's good to meet you, Joy," the doctor said, and his voice was deep and rich enough for him to have a career on radio.

"I'm glad to meet you too. Have you seen Connor today?"

"We were just going up. From what his mother says, he's doing very well." The doctor smiled at Veronica. "I'm afraid our boy is growing up."

"I suppose your study will be ending fairly soon then. Once he's off to school, I mean."

"I hope that won't necessarily be the end," Dr. Dahlman said. "He's still a bit young to be on his own, even if he does decide to start college next year. And I'm hoping he'll still be available to work with me if he does leave."

"He has enough credits to finish high school right now," Veronica said, looking as if she was struggling to put on a brave face. "I'm trying to get him to wait at least until June so he can graduate with his classmates. He doesn't seem to think that's important."

"He wants to move on," the doctor said. "Yes, he's young, but he's also practical and focused and eager to stand on his own two feet. Well beyond his age."

A couple with two small children approached the doors, and Dr. Dahlman, asking their pardon, stepped farther away from the exit to let them pass.

"Will you publish your study when it's done?" Joy asked him.

"Oh definitely. Definitely. I've learned a lot, I believe, about how a high level of intelligence affects the maturity of the brain. Of course, none of my conclusions will be worth anything until they can be independently verified. After all these years, I don't want to have to rush the end of the study. I've worked too long on this to have it all invalidated because I missed something in my hurry. And just now I'm studying how the pain medications Connor is taking during his recovery affect his brain. I'm learning a great deal just from that."

He seemed awfully happy about having the opportunity.

"Maybe Connor will stay in high school the rest of the year. Would that be long enough?"

Dr. Dahlman sighed. "I'd like to keep him another year after that at least. Another five or ten even would be better, but he's a determined young man. Even having till June would let me at least have the opportunity to prepare some of my conclusions and test them for a short time. Ah, but we have to take what is available to us. I knew a boy like Connor would want to spread his wings before very much longer anyway."

"It's what we prepare them for all their lives, isn't it?"

"But it's never easy when the time comes," Veronica said wistfully.

The doctor patted her shoulder. "He's not leaving today, you know. Come on. We'd better go see him before he decides he's going to hobble out the front door."

Veronica's eyes widened. "Oh, he wouldn't."

"No, no, of course not. Now come on." Dr. Dahlman turned to Joy. "It was good meeting you, Joy. I know Veronica is glad you came up to see Connor. It's nice to have a good neighbor or two in tough times."

"It certainly is," Joy said. "Veronica, I'll see you soon."

Joy lived only a short way from the hospital, and she almost never drove to work. She walked toward home now as briskly as she could. Along the way, she took out the list Evelyn had made with ideas for Shirley's birthday present. "Birthday meal" she supposed she ought to call it. Four couples. That would be a nice cozy number. *If* Roger accepted her invitation.

She and Roger were only friends at this point. Part of her liked it that way. It was easy and fun, and neither of them had any expectations. Then again, there wasn't that deep understanding between the two of them that she had missed ever since her husband, Wilson, passed away not even two years ago. Sometimes it seemed like it had happened only yesterday. Other times, as if decades had passed. Wilson could never be replaced, of course, but someone like Roger could certainly be a nice companion. Even a casual date was better than feeling like the odd one out when everyone else was paired up.

As she walked under the palm trees that swayed in the sea-scented air, she thought about what she could get Shirley for her birthday. More than anything, she wished she could give her something better than merely an evening away from her caregiving duties. She knew Shirley loved her mother dearly, but that didn't mean taking care of her wasn't stressful sometimes.

Joy decided she ought to be more deliberate about spending time with Regina herself. She wasn't so busy that she couldn't visit more often and let Shirley have some time for herself. That would be a bigger blessing to Shirley than any tchotchke she could order online and wrap in pretty paper. Though she wanted to get Shirley something like that too.

She breathed in the cooling breeze off the ocean, let it seep into every part of her, and then let it out again, allowing the tension she felt to release along with it. All in all, it had been a productive day. Daisy had worked out her problem with Veronica Sherman, and

Connor Sherman was in the hospital, if one had to be there at all, for something not too serious. He was showing his mother that he was healthy and strong and ready to face the world. Besides that, Joy's idea for surprising Shirley with a birthday dinner had been received with enthusiasm, and everyone so far was on board. All she had to do was make sure Roger was available that evening and then make the reservations. There was really nothing for her to be tense about in the first place.

When she got home, she went through her mail and then made herself a crisp, cool garden salad for dinner. Then she got comfortable on the couch and called Roger, not sure whether or not he'd have time to talk. She never knew what his schedule was going to be like.

He was in charge of awarding the charitable donations from his family's paper manufacturing business, and that meant he spent a lot of time socializing and meeting with various organizations who could benefit from the company's help. He was often invited to their fundraising functions and to whatever else they might have going on that raised awareness for whatever cause they supported. She was almost surprised when he answered the call on the second ring.

"Joy," he said. "I was just thinking of calling you."

"That's a nice coincidence. I hope that means I've caught you at a convenient time."

"Definitely. What's going on?"

"I'd like to ask you something, but now I'm curious. Why were you going to call me?"

"I only wanted to catch up with you. Seems like I've been all over the place lately, and I haven't seen you around much." He paused for a beat. "I was wondering if you might like to go to dinner or something sometime soon."

"Actually, I would. That's why I was calling you."

"Oh, really? Sounds like we're on then."

"This is kind of a special dinner. It wouldn't be only us, but it would be for an excellent cause."

"Sounds like something I have a lot of experience with."

"But I don't want you to feel like you have to go if you'd rather not," Joy said quickly. "We can always do something else another time, if you like."

"You should at least tell me what it is before you try to convince me not to go."

She laughed at that. "I'd love you to go, if you'd like to."

"Try me."

"Okay. You know my friend Shirley from the hospital. The twentieth is her birthday. That's Tuesday. Evelyn, Anne, and I were talking about having a little get-together for her. Nothing big or anything, but we thought it might be a fun surprise to take her to a nice place for dinner and have James and Ralph and Garrison be there to surprise her. And I thought maybe you'd like to be there too."

Joy hoped that came across as friendly and casual and not desperate.

"That sounds fun," Roger said. "I'd like to come. You said the twentieth? Let me check my calendar. Hang on."

He was silent for a moment, and she imagined him scrolling through the calendar on his phone.

"The only thing I have that day," he said finally, "is a lunch for one of the animal shelters we support. No reason I can't have dinner with you and the birthday girl."

"Great. I'm glad you can come. And, really, I don't have much going on besides that, if you'd like to have dinner some other time too."

"Just us?" he asked, a touch of teasing in his voice.

"Just us."

"I was thinking this coming Saturday if you don't have any other plans."

"I'd love that. I'm free."

"Great, so we're on?"

"Definitely. Are we talking casual? Dressy?"

"Whatever you think," Roger said, "though after all the tuxes I have to wear to all the events I've been to, something a little more relaxed would be nice."

"Fine with me. Jeans and a hamburger would work for me."

"You're the best, Joy. We might not have to be quite as relaxed as that, but it does sound good."

"Surprise me," she told him, thinking how nice it would be to spend time with him without there being anything special going on. "As long as I know what to put on, I'm up for it."

"That's a deal. Exactly how formal is this get-together for Shirley supposed to be?"

"You don't need to wear a tux, but it is at Revival, so you probably shouldn't show up in sweats or anything."

"Something between sweats and a tux. Got it."

"Ahem. How about nice but not formal?"

"I can do that too," he promised. "Do we know what time yet?"

"I wanted to talk to you before I made any reservations, but that's my next step. Can I text you with details?"

"Absolutely. I haven't met Evelyn's husband yet, but I know Garrison and Ralph. I'm sure we'll all have plenty to talk about."

"Great," Joy said. "I'll get back to you about Tuesday, and you let me know about Saturday."

"I'm looking forward to it. Talk to you soon."

"Good night."

She smiled as she hung up the phone. Talking to him always seemed to have that effect on her.

A few minutes later she had made a reservation for eight at Revival for the twentieth at seven o'clock. She even reserved their small private dining room. Afterward, she sent texts with the pertinent information to Evelyn, Anne, Garrison, and Roger. That done, she sat down at her computer and started looking for a special gift for Shirley.

***

Joy got to the hospital before seven the next morning as she usually did and spent the next hour enjoying the gourmet coffee she always brewed up in the gift shop's back room. She was glad too that she had reached the hospital before the hard rain that now thrummed against the lobby's windows began. She had heard back from Garrison and Roger about the birthday dinner, but there was nothing so far from Evelyn or Anne. She considered calling them both up and asking them to have coffee with her again, but then she decided they probably had plenty to deal with without her bothering them at this point. It was very early yet. They'd probably get back to her before much longer anyway.

She thought about Connor Sherman too and wondered how much longer he'd be in the hospital. Hopefully, there wouldn't be any more dustups between Veronica and Daisy, and he'd get the green light to go back home and carry on with his life. He may have even gone home by now. She hadn't thought to ask. She decided she'd drop by his room again if she happened to be up that way sometime during the day. It would be nice to check on Veronica too. She was definitely going to need a friend once Connor eventually left home.

The gift shop ended up being busy during the early part of the day, so Joy didn't have much time to wonder about Shirley's birthday or about Connor and his mother. She didn't think about them at all, in fact, even when her longtime volunteer, Lacy, came in to work. Not until the gift shop phone rang.

"Mercy Hospital gift shop," Joy said when she answered it. "This is Joy."

"Joy."

The voice on the other end of the line was unsteady, almost tearful. It took her a moment to recognize it.

"Veronica?"

"Yes. It's Veronica. Oh Joy, I'm sorry to bother you. I know you're working. But could you possibly come up to Connor's room? I'm so upset."

"What's wrong?"

Joy glanced over at Lacy as she set out a display of Halloween items. Lacy stopped what she was doing, eyeing Joy with concern.

"I'm not sure," Veronica sobbed, "but I think somebody is trying to make Connor sick."

Chapter Four

"Is Connor okay?" Joy asked. "Veronica?"

Veronica sniffled into the phone. "I think he will be. Dr. Morton is seeing him right now, but I'm so upset. He sent me to the waiting room until he gets Connor settled."

Probably because she was making things worse.

"But what happened?" she asked.

"Can you come talk to me? Only for a few minutes, I promise. I think I know, but I need to talk to somebody about it before I say anything to the staff here. I thought I was wrong about that girl yesterday, but now I'm not so sure."

"Actually, my assistant Lacy came in only a few minutes ago, so I can come up. As long as I don't stay away too long."

"Oh, thank you. I have to talk to somebody before I go completely crazy."

"All right. I'll be right there. Try to stay calm. I'm sure Dr. Morton will do whatever he can to make sure Connor will be okay."

Once she hung up the phone, Joy told Lacy what was going on and asked her to look after the shop for a few minutes. That done, Joy quicky made her way to the elevator and went to the second floor.

She found Veronica pacing in the hallway in front of her son's closed door.

"Oh, Joy." Veronica rushed to her and grasped her hand. "I'm so glad to see you."

"I thought you were in the waiting room."

"That's where Dr. Morton told me to go, but I couldn't stand it in there by myself."

"Come on." Joy took her arm. "Let's sit down and have some coffee, and you can tell me about it."

Veronica nodded, seeming calmer already, and she went with Joy to sit down. Joy got her a cup of coffee, and they settled on one of the love seats that faced the window.

"Drink a little of that," Joy told her, and Veronica obediently took a few sips. "Okay now. Tell me what happened."

Veronica clutched her cup in both hands. "I don't want to make any accusations, but after what happened yesterday…"

"Are you saying you think Daisy did something to Connor?"

"I'm not sure, but I don't know who else it could have been."

"Who else what could have been?" Joy asked. "Why don't you start from the beginning and tell me what happened?"

"Okay." Veronica took a steadying breath. "Last night, Dr. Morton said there was only one more test he wanted to run on Connor. He said he scheduled it for this morning, and that unless he found something he wasn't expecting when he examined Connor's knee, Connor and I could go home right afterward."

"And what happened?"

"Well, I went home last night. I used to always sleep in Connor's room when he had to be hospitalized, but he put a stop to that over a year ago. He said that unless he was actually sick, really sick, he could handle spending the night on his own. So I left. I called him this morning, but he didn't answer, so I called the nurses' station. They said he was getting his test done, and he should be through later on."

"So they gave you no reason to be concerned."

"Not at all. I should have been with him anyway, I know. I'll never forgive myself for not being here."

"Veronica," Joy said firmly. "Tell me what happened."

"Well, I thought it was all routine, so I did some things I've been meaning to do around the house and then I went to the grocery store to pick up what we were out of. I had just put away what needed to be refrigerated when my phone rang. It was Fanny, from the nurses' station. She said Connor had had an allergic reaction. She told me Dr. Morton was taking care of it, but she said she knew I'd want to come up to the hospital."

"Oh no. What did he have a reaction to?"

"Evidently somebody had delivered some flowers downstairs and one of the volunteers brought them up while Connor was napping. Katie says he was watching TV after his test was over and fell asleep, so nobody realized he was having a reaction until he woke up and couldn't breathe."

"And the doctor wouldn't let you see him?"

Veronica winced. "It's not that exactly. I came up to the room after Dr. Morton had already given him something to counteract the allergen, but I guess I was so upset about not being here when those flowers were delivered, I was making Connor upset too. The doctor said I would be able to see Connor in a few minutes. But that's why I needed to talk to someone right away. How can I calm down when I know I could have prevented this whole thing from happening? I know he's allergic to certain flowers. I would never have let them be brought into the room."

"The nurses aren't aware of that particular allergy?" Joy asked.

"I'm sure it's in his records, but I don't think anybody noticed when the flowers were delivered."

"Do they know who delivered them?"

Veronica's eyes filled with tears, not tears of sorrow but of anger. "The flowers were daisies. It had to have been that Daisy Graham again."

"You can't blame her simply because she has the same name as the flowers," Joy said, reminding herself how upset the woman was. "And even if Daisy did bring them up to Connor's room, that's part of her job. It doesn't mean she sent them."

"What about this?"

Veronica took a small envelope from her purse. It had the name and logo of a local florist on it. Inside the envelope was a little yellow card with flowers and ribbons along the edges. On it was written *Get well soon*. There was no signature.

"Do you recognize the writing?" Joy asked her.

"No, but look at it. It's the same kind of rounded, childish writing a lot of girls her age use."

"Still—"

"Look," Veronica said with forced calm. "I don't want to make any wild accusations, but she is in competition with Connor for that scholarship their school gives out, and from what I can tell, her family doesn't have the ability to send her to a good college without some kind of help. Maybe she wants to keep him from graduating this year and being valedictorian. The incident with the mail was bad enough, but this could have been very serious."

"I realize that. But you'd have to have some actual proof if you were going to press charges."

"Oh, I don't want to do that." Veronica's sternness faded. "If it was Daisy, and yes, I'll admit that I can't positively say it was, I'm sure she didn't think about what the consequences might be. I don't want to get her into trouble over this, but it has to stop, don't you think so?"

"Of course it does," Joy assured her. "And, if you like, I could ask the woman in charge of the volunteers if Daisy delivered those flowers, but couldn't they have been sent by someone else? A family member maybe? A friend? Someone who didn't mean any harm to Connor? Someone who isn't aware he's allergic?"

"If this was unintentional, why wasn't the note signed?"

She had a point there.

"Could I have the card that came with the flowers?" Joy asked. "I'd like to see what the florist says about the person who sent it, and there are some other questions I'd like to ask too."

"Questions you'd like to ask Daisy?" Veronica asked.

"To be honest, yes. I'd like to rule her out, if I can. Either way, I want to know for sure what happened. Is there a particular reason you think it has to be her?"

"I don't suppose it has to be her," Veronica said reluctantly, "but I don't know who else would have it out for Connor. Certainly nobody here at the hospital."

"Really, it could have been totally unintentional. So what do you think? Do you want me to talk to her?"

"That sounds fair." Veronica handed Joy the envelope with the card in it. "I'm afraid I might not be very diplomatic if I asked her about this. And really, all I want is to make sure my son is safe, you know?"

Before Joy could respond, Dr. Morton came into the waiting room. He was a tall, slender young Black man, well respected at the hospital. He gave Joy a slight smile.

"Good to see you, Joy."

"Hello, Dr. Morton. How are you? How's Connor?"

"He's going to be fine."

Veronica sagged in her chair. "Thank God. When can I see him?"

"He's resting right now, Mrs. Sherman. And you and I need to have a little talk before you go in there anyway."

Veronica bit her lip.

"I'd better get back to work," Joy said, standing up.

Veronica looked at her, her eyes pleading, but Dr. Morton nodded.

"I think that would be best, Joy."

"I just stopped by because Veronica wanted somebody to talk to. She and I are neighbors."

"I didn't know that. I'm glad you could be here for her."

"I'll see you later, Doctor. Veronica, I'll have that conversation we were talking about. If there's anything that comes of it, I'll call you."

"Yes, please do," Veronica said.

"I will. I'm glad Connor's all right."

"Me too. Now I guess you'd better let Dr. Morton get on with scolding me."

The doctor's expression warmed. "No scolding, Mrs. Sherman, but we do need to talk."

"Then I'll see you both later."

Joy left the waiting room half wishing she were a fly on the wall and could hear what Dr. Morton had to say without being observed. Still, she needed to find Daisy, tell her what was going on, and get her side of the story. By the time she got down to the lobby, she ran into Mandy, one of the other volunteers, and found out that Daisy had just taken a vase full of roses to the patient in Room 403. Joy got back on the elevator and went to the fourth floor. Daisy was coming down the hall pushing an elderly woman in a wheelchair.

"Hi, Joy," Daisy said with her usual bright smile.

"I was just looking for you." Joy nodded at the patient. "Hello."

The woman in the wheelchair gave her a vague smile.

"Mrs. Durham is leaving us today and going back home," Daisy explained.

"That's great. Mind if I tag along for discharge?"

Daisy was clearly puzzled, but she didn't object. "Mrs. Durham's family is already waiting for us, so this shouldn't take long."

They took the patient down to her waiting loved ones and stood at the curb until they drove away.

"What is it?" Daisy asked once she had returned the wheelchair to the station near the door. "You look like you have bad news."

"Let's find a place to talk for a minute."

Joy took her to the back room in the gift shop. Joy didn't want Lacy overhearing anything or thinking that Daisy was in some kind of trouble. They sat down at the table, and Daisy politely declined when Joy offered her coffee.

"It's not my family, is it?" Daisy asked finally. "There wasn't an accident or something, was there?"

"Oh no. No." Joy patted her hand. "Nothing like that."

"Well, that's good."

"Did you take some flowers up to Connor Sherman's room today?"

"Yeah. Why?"

"There was a problem with them."

"The flowers? I don't understand."

"Tell me what you did."

Daisy frowned at her. "Like I always do. Ms. Kingston told me some flowers had been delivered for his room, so I took them up to him. I tapped on the door, but it was already open, so I went in. He was asleep, so I left the flowers on his bed table so he'd see them when he woke up. Then I came back down and went to help in the nursery." Her face lit. "I like holding the babies."

Joy couldn't help smiling too. "They are sweet, but what about Connor?"

Daisy shrugged. "That's all that happened. I hadn't seen him today, not until then. And I haven't seen him since. Actually, before I took up the flowers, I hadn't seen him since I went to talk to his mom about that letter I found in the waiting room. To be honest, I didn't want to go up there today in the first place. I mean, Mrs. Sherman and I worked things out, but I could tell she was still wondering about me, so I was trying to make myself scarce."

"Why didn't you have somebody else take the flowers up for you?"

Daisy's pink cheeks turned pinker. "Uh, everybody else was busy. I heard Connor was out having tests and his mom was at home, so I thought it would be okay to put the flowers in his room and then leave. I didn't think it would be a problem. I still don't understand. *Is* it a problem?"

"It probably shouldn't have been. Did you know Connor is allergic to daisies?"

"No. Oh man, did they make him sick?"

"He had a bad reaction, but Dr. Morton took care of it."

"And his mom thinks I did that on purpose? Oh man."

"I told her it wasn't very likely, and I think Dr. Morton is calming her down."

"I didn't do anything." Daisy's lips quivered. "I promise."

"It's okay. Connor's going to be all right. I imagine he'll have to stay here for the night now, but the doctor seemed more concerned about how his mother was taking it than Connor's recovery."

"I can imagine she was pretty upset. He says she has a fit if he so much as sneezes."

"I understand it can be hard to let your children grow up," Joy said, thinking of her own daughter, "but it must be especially hard in Mrs. Sherman's case. Her daughter's away at school, and Connor is pretty much the only one she has around usually."

"I guess she's going to have to be without him too before too much longer. I can tell Connor's had enough of being smothered by her."

"I know he loves his mom," Joy said, "but it's normal to want more freedom as you grow up."

She thought of the little card she had tucked into her purse. It would be helpful to have a sample of Daisy's writing to compare to it. It would be an easy way to prove to Veronica that Daisy wasn't trying to sabotage her son.

"Well, I'd better get back to work. Lacy is probably wondering where I am right now."

"Yeah," Daisy said. "I'm supposed to go read to Mr. Billingsly. He recently had cancer surgery, and he's mostly blind anyway."

"That's too bad. You have to be in a lot of different places all day, don't you?"

"Most of the time, but I like it. I don't like being stuck at one job for hours at a time."

"Do you have to sign in and out from different stations or anything like that?"

Daisy giggled. "No. That would drive me crazy. We do have to sign in and out when we go on and off duty though."

"That makes sense. Well, you'd better not keep Mr. Billingsly waiting. He's probably bored to tears right now."

"One of the nurses said he ought to get audiobooks, but I think he's a little lonely too. I'm glad to go sit with him for a while. He's nice."

"Off you go then. I'll talk to you later."

Daisy headed out to the lobby and was soon gone.

Joy took out the little card Veronica had given her. *Get well soon.* It certainly would be helpful to compare the writing on it to something Daisy had written, and the volunteer sign-in sheet might be exactly what Joy needed.

Joy was glad to see that things in the shop were running smoothly. It wasn't a very busy day, so she and Lacy had time to chat off and on. With a few casual questions, Joy found out a little more about the volunteers who were working at the hospital right now and how they all got along. When it was time for her to leave for the day, Joy stopped by where Aurora Kingston worked at the reception desk in the lobby. Aurora was the one who coordinated the work of all the volunteers. The volunteer on duty that day was busy helping a visitor locate the patient he was looking for, but there was a clipboard on the desk. It was the volunteers' sign-in sheet.

Joy took a quick look around to make sure nobody would notice and then took out the card and held it close to Daisy Graham's signature on the sign-in sheet. The handwriting on both looked very much alike.

Chapter Five

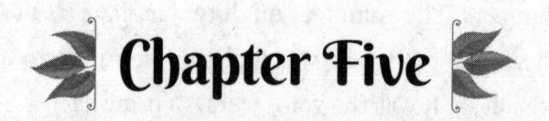

"Joy?"

Joy turned guiltily from the lobby's reception desk, and then relief flooded through her. "Shirley. You scared me to death."

Shirley chuckled. "You look like you're up to no good."

"I was afraid you were Aurora, and I sure didn't want her to think there was something more for her to be hyper about."

"Something going on?" Shirley lowered her voice. "Anything tasty?"

"Oh, I don't know. I think I just found out something I didn't want to."

Shirley raised her eyebrows expectantly.

"Look at this." Joy showed her the card. "Does this card look like it was written by the same person who signed here?"

Shirley studied the card and the signature for a moment. "It does to me. Especially the *G* in *Get well soon* and the *G* in *Graham*. They're curled more like a six than a *G*, don't you think?"

"Exactly. But the handwriting is almost more like printing than cursive, with only a few loops to join the letters."

"A lot of girls write that way, don't they?"

Joy nodded. "But right now, I'm concerned about one girl in particular."

"Daisy? Why? She seems really nice."

"I know." Joy looked around again. Aurora was bound to come back any time now. "Are you in a hurry?"

"I have to take these to the lab," Shirley said with a nod toward the tray of vials she carried, "but then I'm on break. Want to have coffee?"

"I'd love to."

"Your place?"

"No," Joy said. "I don't want Lacy to overhear anything, especially about another volunteer. Can we stop at the Grove?"

"Fine with me."

Joy went with Shirley to the lab, and then they headed for the Grove. They met Anne and Evelyn on the way.

"Hey," Evelyn said. "We were looking for you in the gift shop."

Anne nodded. "I told her you were probably gone for the day, and Lacy said you were."

"We ran into each other and stopped to have a chat." Joy looked at Shirley. "What do you think? Should we let them come too?"

Shirley studied the other two for a moment with exaggerated uncertainty. "If you think they can be trusted. This is a pretty important case."

At once, Anne and Evelyn both looked interested.

"There's a case?" Evelyn asked.

"There have been a couple of minor incidents, unless you count why the person in question is here in the first place," Joy said. "But you two might be able to help us make some sense of what's been happening."

The four of them got coffee and sat down at a quiet table in the corner of the shop. Joy quickly brought them all up to speed on what had been going on with Connor Sherman.

"You think somebody could have put that camera bag deliberately in his way?" Anne asked.

"I'm not saying I know that," Joy told her, "but it's possible. If someone really is trying to sideline Connor, that would be one way to do it."

"But Daisy was nowhere around at the time, was she?" Evelyn asked.

"No," Joy said. "Not that I know of. Only the neighbor boys and the filmmaker and, I'm sure, Connor's mom."

"And you don't have much to go on with those flowers," Shirley said.

"I'm not a handwriting expert," Joy admitted. "But if Daisy didn't write that card, somebody meant it to look that way."

Shirley paused, deep in thought. "I don't think Daisy's the type, but I suppose she could be. But why would anybody want it to look like she was?"

"That's easy," Evelyn told her. "To take the blame in place of the real culprit."

"That's what I think," Anne said. "And if Daisy is actually behind all this, she's pretty clumsy about it. And every time I've been around her, she's seemed like such a sweet, responsible girl."

"She's still young," Joy reminded her. "But this whole handwriting thing is pretty unsettling. Where would somebody get an example of Daisy's writing?"

"That volunteer roster for a start," Shirley said.

Joy shook her head. "Only a start. Wait a minute."

She took pen and pad of paper out of her purse and wrote *Get well soon* and *Daisy Graham*.

"Just as I thought." She marked out the only letters the two phrases had in common, *G* and *S*. "If someone is mimicking Daisy's handwriting, either most of the writing in *Get well soon* is wrong or our perpetrator got a sample from somewhere besides our list of volunteers."

Anne rested her chin in both hands, her forehead puckered. "We know Daisy put those flowers in Connor's room, but that doesn't mean she sent them. Have you checked with the florist?"

"Not yet. I was thinking of stopping by after work. Wouldn't the person who ordered the flowers have to have written out the card and given it to the florist to include when the flowers were delivered?"

"It could have been someone at the florist's. It might have been a phone order, and the card was dictated."

"It could have been Daisy." Evelyn narrowed her eyes. "She could have slipped in the card while she was taking the flowers up to Connor's room."

"Possibly." Joy considered the possibilities. "If the flowers were actually sent by someone else, she could have replaced the card that came with them with the one she wrote, but then she would have had to know what florist sent them in the first place. And what about the person who actually sent them? Wouldn't that person be wondering if Connor got the flowers?"

"Maybe," Anne said. "And if Daisy switched out the cards for some nefarious reason, the original sender would have to have been unaware that Connor was allergic to daisies."

Shirley nodded. "Unless there's more than one person out to get him."

"And, if someone else did send the daisies," Joy said, "why would Daisy put in a note of her own? She wouldn't have been a suspect at all, and she would have gotten the result she wanted anyway."

"I think you ought to ask the people at the florist's about it," Anne said firmly. "That will likely clear the whole thing up."

"It was probably unintentional anyway," Evelyn added. "It sounds like Mom is overprotective and even a little paranoid."

"Definitely overprotective," Joy said. "I don't know about paranoid, but she seems to be a worrier if nothing else."

Shirley pursed her lips. "She's going to drive that boy away if she's not careful."

"I can't say I disagree." Joy sighed. "Well, I'll go to the florist and see what I can find out and let y'all know tomorrow. I just want to make sure we're all on the same page for Shirley's birthday Tuesday night."

She gave Anne and Evelyn a glance, and they each nodded. Things were lining up for the party.

"Garrison did end up asking me out," Shirley said nonchalantly. "We're going to dinner and a concert."

"That's great," Joy told her, pretending she didn't know about it before now. "Do we need to reschedule our dinner?"

"No, the concert is Saturday, so we're good to go."

"And you have someone to look after your mom that night?"

"All set," Shirley said with a smile. "I promised that she and I would do something together too, but we haven't decided what yet."

"That'll be fun," Anne told her.

"I think so." Shirley checked her watch and sighed. "I guess I'd better get back to work before somebody hunts me down."

"Oh wow," Evelyn said, "I'd better go too. We had a mix-up in some medical records that were sent, and we're trying to figure out what happened so it doesn't happen again."

"I'm fine to chat for a bit," Anne said.

"Well, some of us have to work anyway," Shirley said, and then she smiled. "I'll see you girls later on."

"See you," Evelyn said, and they both hurried off.

"So," Anne said when they were gone, "Garrison's on board for Tuesday night too?"

Joy nodded. "Definitely. I didn't want to upset their plans if they were already doing something, but he said he really wanted to take her to that concert, so it worked out perfectly."

"What about her mom?"

"I was wondering that myself," Joy said. "I meant to ask you and Evelyn. Do you think Shirley wants her mom there? Or would she rather do something special for just the two of them?"

"I know what you mean. And it's kind of hard to know without asking what Shirley would actually want." Anne thought for a minute. "She said she already arranged for someone to be with her mom on Tuesday night, right? What if we invite Regina *and* her companion to come to dinner? What do you think?"

"That might be the perfect solution. We'll see if Regina wants to come."

"Hmm." Anne tapped the edge of her coffee cup with one fingernail. "Okay, do you know who will be staying with Regina?"

"She has a couple of different ones. I'd have to see if I can find out without Shirley suspecting anything."

"I'm sure you can handle it." Anne said. "Right now, I'd better get moving. Ralph picked Addie up from school, and he's taking her to the dinosaur museum, just the two of them."

"We have a dinosaur museum?"

"Well, the museum of natural history. Addie's very interested in 'how old people lived.' I told her she could just watch me."

Joy laughed.

"And I promised to make hot dogs and macaroni and cheese and chocolate cake for when they get home. I've got to get to the grocery store." Anne stood up. "Let me know what the people at the florist say. As well as what you find out about Regina. It's going to be a great party."

"We'll make sure it is. For now, I'd better get to the florist and see what they can tell me."

Joy checked the address on the card one more time and then looked up at the sign on the front of the shop. It wasn't the closest florist to the hospital. It wasn't even in the top three. That was a little fishy right off the bat. Somebody was trying to cover a trail.

Joy parked and walked up the cracked sidewalk to the front door. The shop looked as if it had been built sometime in the 1920s. The two bay windows that flanked the front door were full of a colorful variety of flowers, and she smiled at the aqua and white octagonal tiles that spelled out HANSON'S FLORIST in stylish art deco letters that, though they were well kept, looked original to the place. Maybe they'd been carefully replaced over the years.

She went inside and found the woman behind the counter, plump and fiftyish with lines at the corners of her eyes that said she smiled often and laughed more. She wore an old-fashioned shopkeeper apron with the store's art deco name embroidered in aqua on the bib, and she was in the middle of arranging a vase of white roses and violets.

"Welcome to Hanson's," she said as soon as Joy came inside. "I'm Trella. How can I help you?"

Joy inhaled deeply, her eyes closing of their own accord. "Those smell heavenly. And they look gorgeous too."

"Thank you. I'd be happy to make you an arrangement exactly like it."

"Actually," Joy said, "I'm hoping you have a very good memory."

Trella's hazel eyes twinkled. "I remember names better than faces, and I usually remember the orders that go with the names. I hope there's not a problem with something we sent out."

"No, I think the daisies were fine. I'm curious, though, about who sent them. The card wasn't signed."

Joy handed the card to Trella and gave her Connor's name and the name of the hospital.

"That's one of ours, no doubt," Trella said.

"Do you remember if the person who bought the flowers wrote the card here?"

"Oh definitely. She would have had to in order to get it sent over with the flowers."

"I manage the hospital gift shop, and I was wondering if you remember when that was?"

"This morning." Trella scrunched up her forehead as she thought. "Ten or ten thirty, I'd say."

"Do you remember the person who ordered the flowers?" Joy asked feeling a little frisson of excitement. "It was a woman?"

"Yes, but I didn't know her. I'm almost positive she hadn't been in here before."

Joy nodded, trying to urge the woman on. "What was she like? Can you describe her?"

"It was raining over here this morning, pretty hard actually. She came in wearing a raincoat, one of those cloth ones, and had a scarf over her head. Oh, and glasses. The heavy-looking horn-rimmed ones. Mona took her order because I was making up some arrangements for a rehearsal dinner. The woman ordered daisies, and I stopped what I was doing and made them up while Mona checked her out."

"But what was she like? Young? Old? Short? Tall?"

Trella shrugged. "She didn't say much, and her voice was pretty low. Not old, I don't think, though her clothes weren't exactly the latest thing. They weren't bad, just kind of tired looking, you know? She was white, I remember that much. She wasn't here that long."

"Okay," Joy said. "What name did she give you?"

"None. She paid cash, so we didn't really have to have a name. She wrote out the card and gave us the money and then hurried back out into the rain."

"Hmm." Joy showed her the card again. "Would you remember if this was the card she left with you?"

Trella studied it. "Pretty sure. I know she left a card, and I definitely didn't put a different one on the arrangement. I usually don't pay much attention to the messages people write." She frowned. "Are you sure there wasn't a problem with the daisies?"

"Only a little mystery about who might have sent them," Joy said. "The young man they were sent to might have a secret admirer."

"Ah," Trella said with a chuckle. "Well, we'll be here if anybody needs bridal bouquets."

"Thanks," Joy said. "We'll definitely keep you in mind. And thanks for your help."

Joy stepped back into the street and looked up at the slate-gray sky. The clouds were supposed to clear before too much longer, but it would have been better if this morning had been sunny and dry. The woman who ordered the daisies, whoever she was, had certainly taken advantage of the weather to hide her identity.

Chapter Six

As usual, Joy got to work early the next morning, her to-do list already set out clearly in her head. Besides her actual work duties, there were several things she needed to see to during the day. She needed to tell Shirley, Anne, and Evelyn what she had found out at the florist shop. She needed to find out, very subtly of course, who was scheduled to stay with Shirley's mother on Shirley's birthday. Then she, Evelyn, and Anne needed to decide if they ought to ask Regina and her helper to come to Shirley's party.

She wanted to go upstairs and make sure Connor had completely recovered from yesterday's incident. And she wanted to make sure his mother was doing all right too. Dr. Morton was a kind man, but he was also good about telling people what they actually needed to hear without any soft-pedaling. Joy hoped that, whatever he said to Veronica, it had gotten through.

Most important of all, Joy wanted to sit down with Daisy and ask her a few more questions. Whoever had written that card had written it there in the florist's shop. She hated to think that Daisy really could be behind this, but the handwriting seemed pretty telling.

Shirley stopped by right before the gift shop officially opened and, showing Joy pictures on her phone, she asked her opinion about which dress she ought to buy for Tuesday night. She ended up not making a decision, but she bookmarked several possibilities.

As they chatted, Joy brought up Regina staying at home the night of the birthday dinner. Shirley said she had already arranged for their family friend Dorothy Jones, who went by Dot, to be there with her. Joy had to hide a smile as the conversation turned to the jazz concert Garrison had planned for Saturday, but as soon as Shirley left to start her shift, Joy called Anne and told her what she had found out. They decided having Regina at the party would be a nice surprise, and Joy told Anne she'd call Dot and work out the details. That was something else to add to her mental to-do list.

When Lacy came in to help out at the shop, Joy made her way toward the elevators, planning to go up to see Connor and Veronica. Evelyn intercepted her before she got there.

"Got a second?" she asked.

"Sure. What's up?"

"Anne told me that you were planning to have Shirley's mother come to dinner on Tuesday."

"We thought she might like having her there," Joy said. "Do you think it's a bad idea?"

"Not at all. But, since she's coming, and whoever's taking care of her, what would you think of inviting a couple more people?"

Joy frowned. "Who?"

"A couple of the nurses Shirley works with asked me if anybody was planning anything for her birthday. I didn't want to say anything until I talked to you, so I told them I'd let them know. What do you think? Do we want to invite more people? I'm not saying the whole hospital or anything, but a few of Shirley's friends up here wouldn't hurt, would it?"

"No, but we're talking an actual dinner at a pretty tony place. They'd have to commit to being there, because we'd have to make reservations. Do we know specifically who wants to come, or is this just something people are asking about?"

"I don't know, but Anne said somebody mentioned Shirley's birthday to her too. What do you think?"

"Maybe an actual dinner isn't the best idea. What if we did something more casual? Maybe a buffet?"

Joy considered that. "Might not be a bad idea. It won't be as elegant, but it would still be nice. We'd have to keep it to a reasonable number of people, but I think it would be all right. The more the merrier. What does Anne think?"

"She's all for it, and I agree. How many do you think we can add?"

Joy put another item on her mental to-do list. "Let me call the restaurant and see what they have to offer buffet-wise. If you see Anne, tell her not to say anything to anybody until I figure out what our options are."

"Great. Thanks for taking care of it." Evelyn glanced at her watch. "And it's back to work for me. Talk to you soon."

"All right. I'll let you and Anne know whenever I do."

Joy took the elevator up to the second floor, wondering if, with the potential change of plans, Revival was perhaps not the best choice for this event. Yes, Shirley had enjoyed eating there, and it was one of the nicest places in Charleston, but it was also expensive. She, Anne, and Evelyn hadn't discussed the financial side of this endeavor. Joy had assumed they would all pay their own way and pay for Shirley's meal too. She hated to invite other people to the birthday party and tell them there would be a "so much per person" charge. They needed to figure this out and soon. Tuesday was coming.

She found Veronica with Connor in his room. With them was a striking-looking woman, probably in her midthirties. With her athletic build and tanned skin along with the sun streaks in her abundant, curly brown hair, it seemed likely that she spent a lot of time outdoors, probably doing something adventurous. Joy was certain she knew who this was.

"Joy," Veronica said, "I'm so glad you dropped by. There's someone I'd like you to meet."

Joy offered her hand to the other woman. "You must be Swarna LeFrye. I'm Joy Atkins. I work in the gift shop downstairs."

Swarna turned to take Joy's hand, and the light from the window glinted off the tiny diamond set in the side of her nose.

"Hello," she said, her voice low and even. "I understand you and Veronica are neighbors too."

"We are. I won't interrupt your visit though. I only wanted to see how Connor is today and how the tests are going."

Connor shrugged. "I'm fine now. Ready to go home."

"Not until Dr. Morton says you can," his mother reminded him. "And Dr. Dahlman still has some tests to run too. His were delayed because of what happened yesterday."

Connor sighed. "I have homework to catch up on too."

"You could work on it now," Veronica suggested.

Connor rolled his eyes.

"Knowing you," Swarna said, "you'll have it all done in no time. I'd like to do some filming while you're here, if that's all right with you, ask you about your allergy incident and so on. Dr. Dahlman says you'll be here at least through tomorrow."

"Great," Connor said glumly.

Veronica immediately looked worried. "He didn't tell us that. Did he say something's wrong?"

"Not to me," Swarna told her, "but one of the nurses mentioned it. And I doubt it's anything but more routine tests for his study. Look at Connor. Now that his knee is getting better, he doesn't belong in a hospital any more than I do."

"He's still a little flushed."

Veronica pressed the back of her hand to his cheek, and he pulled away from her.

"Mom."

"Well, I'm sorry, honey. You worried me yesterday. But yes, Swarna's right. You're looking better, and we'll get you home as soon as the doctors say it's okay."

"I understand you've been filming Connor since he was quite small," Joy said to Swarna. "That must be very interesting."

"Definitely. I enjoy long-term projects like that. It's amazing to look back at the early footage and compare it to more recent images. My problem is that Connor is a little too well adjusted. Viewers connect better with characters who have hardships or some kind of flaws. Connor knows what he wants and isn't afraid to reach out and get it."

Joy smiled. "I guess conflict is what makes a good story, but I'd say his success despite some of the difficulties he's faced will make a wonderful story too."

"It's all in how you tell it," Swarna said confidently. "I've entered my films in a lot of competitions for the past several years, but I think this one is going to put me over the top. Once I get it finished, it's going straight to Sundance."

"You mean the big independent film festival in Colorado?"

"Is there any other? If I can get some notice there, hopefully a few awards, I might be able to get some backers and really hit it big."

"Hey," Joy said, "then you'll be a star, Connor."

He wrinkled his nose. "I'll take a hard pass, thanks. I don't mind if you do what you want with the stuff you've filmed already, Swarna, and you can film what you were planning for right now. But I don't think you ever said how long you were planning to keep filming me. Are you about done?"

Swarna's eyes warmed. "I was wondering when I'd get to the end of your patience for this."

"It's only that I don't know why you need more. I'm going to be out of high school before too much longer. June at the very latest. Christmas if I can get Mom to agree."

"Well, yes, you will be graduating before long, but that doesn't mean you are really an adult. Not quite yet. And, the same as it is for Dr. Dahlman, it's important for me to follow you until you're actually grown up. Does that make sense?"

"I suppose. But once I go to college, I don't know if I'm going to have a lot of time for this anymore. Besides, I'm not that interesting."

"Of course you are," Swarna said. "Believe me, once I get the film put together so it really tells your story, it will be fascinating."

"You must be very good if you can make people cry about a willow branch," Joy observed.

Swarna chuckled. "It's all about the story. And editing is everything."

"So, do you *want* me to be more entertaining?" Connor asked. "I mean like have a tantrum over chocolate pudding? Or get arrested or something?"

"Don't you dare," his mother warned. "Your usual ups and downs are enough to keep me running, thank you very much."

Connor gave Swarna a sly grin.

"I guess you had everybody scared yesterday, didn't you?" she asked him. "I'm glad you're okay, but it would have been some great footage if I had been here."

"Well, I'm not doing it again just because you didn't catch it the first time. You lucked out on getting me wrecking my knee."

Swarna smirked. "I guess I'll have to take what I can get. Maybe Dr. Morton will talk to me a little bit about it. For the camera."

"Have you interviewed Dr. Morton a lot for the film?" Joy asked Swarna. He didn't seem at all the type to put up with that sort of thing.

"Not much," Swarna admitted. "Dr. Dahlman is usually the one I go to when I need a medical explanation, but maybe Dr. Morton will give me a sentence or two I can use. He's younger and better looking than Dahlman, and I'd like to have more footage of him." She had a mischievous glint in her eyes. "Don't tell anyone I said that."

Joy shook her head. "Mum's the word. I've been curious though. If you've been filming Connor all this time, you must have other projects you work on too, unless you follow him around every day."

"It only seems like it," Connor murmured.

One corner of Swarna's mouth twitched. "Actually, I always have several things in the works at any given time. Some of them are relatively quick, like a sprint, and I pour everything into them until they're done. Others, like Connor's, are more like marathons. Slow and steady. Of course, there are things I make sure to do each year, right, Connor?"

"Yeah," he said. "Birthdays and Christmas. Beginning of a school year. End of a school year. Don't you think my graduation, whenever it is, would be a great way to end your film?"

"Definitely. If you mean your college graduation. When you get your PhD."

Connor shook his head. "You never give up."

She patted his arm. "You know you're the boss. I'm only trying to get whatever footage I can while I can."

"All right. But fair warning, okay? I'm not doing this forever."

"Fair warning," she agreed. "Are you feeling up to a little bit of filming today? Maybe we can talk about your little incident with the flowers?"

Connor sighed heavily. "I'm supposed to do some more of Dr. Dahlman's tests later on. Can we make it tomorrow or something?"

"Sure. You'll still be here then," Swarna said.

"Seems like it."

There was a knock on the frame of the open door, and Dr. Dahlman came in.

"Hello, everyone. Connor, are you ready to get to work?"

"See what I mean?" Connor said, and then looked at Dr. Dahlman. "Yeah, I guess. Is this going to take a long time?"

"We'll try to make it as brief and painless as possible. Come along."

Connor got out of bed and grabbed his crutches. "I'll see you in a little while."

"Do you want me to come with you?" Veronica asked hopefully. "I won't mind."

"Now, you know that's distracting, Veronica," Dr. Dahlman said. "We've talked about it before."

"Yes, I know." Veronica's voice was wistful. "Maybe you should use a wheelchair, honey."

"I'll be fine, Mom," Connor said. "Why don't you go home and relax? I can call you when I get back. And can you see if Dr. Morton will let me go home tonight?"

"I'll ask, but he knows what's best for you."

"Yeah, I know."

"I think I'll go see if I can talk to Dr. Morton too," Swarna told Connor, "and then I'll come back and see how your tests went. Maybe you'll feel up to being filmed for a little while."

"You know, Swarna—"

"Hey, if you're not, maybe we can set another time, okay?"

"Yeah, okay."

"Goodbye, ladies," Dr. Dahlman said, and he and Connor left the room.

"I suppose I won't get my turn until tomorrow," Swarna said, clearly disappointed. "But I hope Dr. Morton will be a little more cooperative."

"You must have had to learn a lot about medical issues over the course of making this film," Joy said. "I know I get confused about some of the medical terms I hear around here."

A Genius Solution

"It can be confusing," Swarna agreed. "I've had to rely on Connor's doctors to explain things as simply as possible for the film. Sometimes I wish I had at least a little experience with the medical side of things, even first aid or something. It would have come in handy on some of my adventures, but the opportunity never came up. Of course, Connor can tell you everything about any of the issues he's dealing with and probably several others. He soaks up information like a new mop."

"He always has," Veronica said. "So, Swarna, are you really going to try to interview Dr. Morton about the reaction Connor had yesterday?"

"*Try* being the operative word," Swarna told her. "I'm hoping the doctor has had a good day so far."

"I told Connor I'd ask about him getting released tonight too. Mind if I come with you? I won't take up too much of his time."

"Sure. Come on." Swarna smiled at Joy. "It was nice meeting you, Joy."

"And you," Joy said. "Veronica has told me about some of your films. Are they easy to find?"

Swarna shrugged. "They are on some streaming services. *The Branch* is on DVD, but it was put out by a French company, and it's very hard to find here in the States. Some of them are on YouTube, though I'm not very happy about that. They weren't authorized by me, and most of them are broken up into several sections. It ruins the whole continuity of the story, especially when some of the sections can't be found."

"But they're all under your name? Swarna LeFrye?"

"You can just put Swarna, if you like. You're not going to find many Swarnas."

"That sounds easy," Joy said brightly. "Which one would you recommend most? Among the ones I can find on YouTube anyway."

"Hmm. You might start with *Mr. Patterson's Button*. It's relatively short."

"Oh, I liked that one," Veronica put in.

"Or," Swarna added, "if you want something a little less serious, maybe *Arson*."

"That's less serious than the button one?" Joy asked.

Swarna nodded serenely. "You'll have to judge for yourself. That's the whole point of all of them."

"All right. I'll check it out. Do you have a website?"

"Oh yes. It's swarna dot com. How easy is that?"

"Very easy. Thanks."

"It's mostly pictures though, with a few videos. I was a photojournalist before I was a filmmaker, so I put some of my best up for people to see."

"You must have lived an interesting life," Joy observed. "I'd definitely enjoy seeing your pictures."

"I've been on almost every continent and in almost every country in the world. I'm planning to go to Egypt next year. I want to do a documentary on the Nile."

"That should keep you very busy for a while. Are you going to wrap up things with Connor so you can concentrate on that?"

"Oh no," Swarna said. "I've been working on Connor's film for too long to let it end with a thud. I want to get as much as I can on him as long as he'll let me. I can't tell you all of my plans at this point, but I'm sure this one will be the one that gets me over the top after all these years."

"If you're going to get Dr. Morton to give you an interview," Veronica said, "we'd better get moving, don't you think?"

"Absolutely. Joy, nice to meet you. I'll see you around."

"I'd better get back to work now too," Joy said. "And, Veronica, I think Connor's right. You ought to go home and relax awhile. He'll be fine."

"Maybe so," Veronica said uncertainly. "First I'd better check with Dr. Morton. See you later."

"I'll walk with y'all to the elevator," Joy said.

When they got there, Veronica and Swarna went up. Joy went down. As soon as she was through for the day, she was going to see if she could find Daisy and ask her about the card that had come with the flowers she had taken up to Connor Sherman's room.

Chapter Seven

RIGHT WHEN IT WAS TIME for Joy to leave that afternoon, Daisy came into the gift shop looking for something new to read to Mr. Billingsly. She picked out one of Agatha Christie's Poirot novels.

"That's a good one," Joy told her as she rang up a paperback copy of *Curtain*. "But tell Mr. Billingsly to pay attention. It can be a little bit confusing if you don't catch all the clues."

"I'll make sure to tell him that." Daisy grinned. "We have such a good time, especially when we read a mystery. We discuss the clues, and then we have to make a guess before the end of the book about who we think did the crime and why. Mr. Billingsly is so much better at it than I am."

"He's probably read a lot of mysteries before."

"I think so, but he always tells me if he knows the solution ahead of time. Then I have to guess who did it. But he always reminds me of the clues that are important and helps me work it out for myself. I'm going to be sorry when he goes home."

"He sounds like a very nice man," Joy said, but she was thinking the same of Daisy. It was hard to think of this sweet, giving young woman doing something for personal gain that would harm someone else. "Do you mind if I walk with you a little while on your way back to Mr. Billingsly's room? There's something I'd like to talk to you about, and I want to keep it only between us."

Daisy glanced at Lacy, who was checking out an older couple buying a balloon bouquet. "Um, sure. Am I in trouble again? Connor's not worse, is he?"

"No, he's just fine, I think. Why don't we go ahead and go, and we'll talk."

"Sure."

Judging by her expression, Daisy wasn't sure at all.

"I'm headed out, Lacy," Joy said. "See you later."

She and Daisy left the shop and walked through the lobby.

"Do we need to sit down somewhere again?" Daisy asked glumly.

"Well…" Joy winced. "Maybe we do, because I have a favor to ask, and it would help to have a table or something."

They ended up back in the waiting room where they had had their earlier conversation. They sat where they had before. Daisy was perched on the edge of her seat, like a bird ready to take flight.

"What's this about?" she asked.

"I have something I'd like to find out about, and I think you can help me. At least, I think you can help me rule out someone who didn't do anything wrong."

"That would be good." Daisy's expression darkened. "Is this about those flowers again?"

Joy nodded. "Do you mind?"

Daisy shrugged. "Go ahead."

"Here's the deal. I want to rule out anything besides a mistake. It could be that someone sent the flowers not realizing how allergic

Connor would be, in which case, we wouldn't have to worry about something like this happening again."

"And if it wasn't a mistake?" Daisy asked.

"Then I want to make sure nobody gets in trouble except the person responsible. And I want to prevent it from happening again."

"That would be good."

"Okay." Joy opened her purse and took out a pen and a notepad. "First, understand that I'm only trying to get at the truth here, all right?"

Daisy nodded, and Joy put the pad and pen on the square coffee table in front of them.

"Do me a favor and write *Get well soon* on that pad."

Daisy complied, her forehead puckered as she bent over the paper. When she was through, Joy took the pen and notepad from her.

"What is this about?" Daisy asked.

"I was hoping I could show Mrs. Sherman that your handwriting doesn't look anything like what's on the card that came with them."

"Does it?"

Joy took the little card out of her purse and put it and the notepad back on the coffee table in front of Daisy. They were nearly identical.

"It wasn't me." Daisy's eyes filled with tears. "I promise it wasn't me. I don't know anything about this card, and I didn't write it."

"I'm not saying you did, but I was hoping this might be a good indication that you didn't."

This was puzzling. Joy knew that just because Daisy seemed sweet, it didn't mean she was innocent. But if she had written that card, she had known before now what was written on it. Joy knew too, at least in Veronica Sherman's eyes, that Daisy was the chief suspect. But if Daisy was guilty, wouldn't she have at least tried to change her handwriting a little bit when she was asked for a sample? Wasn't the similarity of the two pieces of writing a clue that actually worked in her favor?

Daisy grabbed a tissue from the little box on the table and quickly blotted her eyes. "This doesn't make sense to me. I wouldn't hurt anybody. Not on purpose."

"And you really didn't know Connor is allergic to daisies?"

"No. I mean we've known each other for a while now, at school and stuff, but he doesn't usually talk about whatever problems he has. I heard that he had a lot of medical problems when he was growing up, and that was what one of the other volunteers said after he came up here. If he says much of anything to me, it's usually about what he's planning to do once he gets into college."

"What about you? I know you want to go to college."

"I do," Daisy admitted. "But there's really no money for it. Dad works hard, and Mom stays home with my younger brothers and sisters, so there's not a lot of extra. And I don't want them worrying about me. If I can't get a good scholarship, I'll have to work for a while and try to save up the money."

"How many brothers and sisters do you have?"

"Three sisters and two brothers. The oldest two after me are in middle school. The next two are in grade school still, and then Richie is supposed to start preschool next year. Mom and Dad figured it would cost more than Mom could earn to have daycare for everybody who needed it. And she didn't want to miss all of us growing up, at least the early years. I know I was always glad she was there for me when I was little."

"So what about scholarships?" Joy asked. "Have you had any good offers?"

"I've applied, and I've gotten some invitations to campuses, but that's all so far. I haven't visited any yet. I know it's early for that, but I wanted to get started as soon as I could."

"You must have a good GPA."

Daisy shrugged. "Yeah. Unless something bad happens, I'll be salutatorian."

"Very nice. But why not valedictorian? You must be close, and it's only September yet."

"No. Nobody's close to Connor. He's miles ahead of everybody else."

"So he'll be the valedictorian this spring. Has he always been at the head of the class?"

"I don't know about always," Daisy said. "He got moved up to my year when I was in eighth grade. And yeah, he's pretty much been ahead ever since."

"How does he do around his classmates? Does he have a lot of friends?"

"He's all right. A lot of the really popular girls, you know the cheerleader types, and the boys who are big in sports and things, they don't pay any attention to him. He's kind of shy, but he's friendly enough with anybody who makes an effort to talk to him. He doesn't like group projects though."

Joy smiled a little. "Why's that?"

"I don't blame him. I don't like them either. You end up doing all the work because otherwise it won't be done right, but then everybody gets the same grade."

"Did you ever work on a project with him?"

"A few times. I think he gets a little frustrated sometimes because everything is so easy for him and people aren't as quick to follow what he's talking about. But he's naturally smart. He can't help that. And he can be pretty funny if he feels comfortable with you."

"Does he feel comfortable with you?" Joy asked.

Daisy looked down at her lap. "I don't know. He doesn't say much when I'm around. He used to more, but last semester, when we came back to school after Christmas, he acted like he didn't want to be around me. I don't think I did anything to hurt his feelings or anything like that. I mean, he's still nice, but he's not the way he was. I don't know why."

"He's had a lot going on, with Dr. Dahlman's studies and the film being made about him and all that."

"Maybe. It doesn't matter anyway."

Daisy still didn't make eye contact. What didn't she want Joy to know?

"Does Connor's mom think I'm trying to do something to Connor?"

"I think she doesn't know who else to blame, but she realizes she doesn't have any proof."

"There's that," Daisy said, nodding toward the notepad still on the coffee table.

"And you don't have any explanation for how that could be so much like the writing on the card?"

"I don't."

"Who would be familiar with your handwriting? Would Connor?"

"Maybe. But he wouldn't have sent those flowers to himself, would he?"

"No, I'm sure he didn't." Joy didn't tell Daisy about her visit to the florist's shop. "Is there anybody up here at the hospital who might see a lot of your writing?"

"Not really. I sign in and stuff, but that's all. It's not enough of a sample for somebody to be able to imitate this."

"You've never written a note to Connor or anything? At school?"

"Of course not." There was an extra tinge of pink in Daisy's cheeks. "Why would I write him a note? I told you, he's just a kid."

"Okay," Joy said carefully, wondering if she might be protesting a little too much, "it's not a big deal. I don't know who wrote the note or why the handwriting looks like yours, but at this point it's not a big deal."

Once more, Daisy nodded toward the notepad. "Are you going to show that to Mrs. Sherman?"

"I was going to if the writing didn't match yours. I told you I wanted to be able to rule you out, but this isn't going to do that."

"Couldn't you have a handwriting expert analyze it or something? I promise it's not my writing even if it looks like it."

"For now, I think I'll hang on to these." Joy picked up the notepad and the card and put them back into her purse. "The important thing at this point is for nothing like this to happen again. If it doesn't, then there's no reason to worry about this."

Daisy slumped in her chair. "You think I'm guilty."

"I don't have any way of knowing," Joy admitted. "I can't imagine that you would have done something like this. I hope you didn't. But I don't have any proof either way. It does sound like you're under a lot of pressure to get a good scholarship, and it could be tempting to do something to level the competition a little, especially when you might think what you did wasn't all that dangerous in the first place. But allergic reactions can end up being quite serious."

"I know that. I'm sorry you don't believe me."

"I want to believe you. I really do. That's why I had you write on the pad. I'm trying to keep an open mind, even though I didn't get the result I hoped to see. And I'm not going to show this to Connor's mother, okay? Not until I find out more, because I don't think you did it, even though I couldn't really rule you out. But if anything else happens to Connor, I'm going to have to bring this up too."

Daisy lifted her chin. "That's okay. I don't have anything to hide."

"All right." Joy reached over and squeezed her hand. "Please understand. I want us to be friends. I'm only trying to help."

"I understand." Daisy managed a small smile and squeezed back. "It doesn't look very good for me, does it?"

"If you didn't do it, then you don't have to worry. I'm going to find out what happened if I can."

"Can I do anything to help? I don't want anyone to hurt Connor either. He…well, he doesn't deserve that. He's a nice kid."

"He is." Joy stood up and brought Daisy with her. "Now you'd better get going. Mr. Billingsly is going to think you ran off with his copy of *Curtain*."

"Thanks," Daisy said, ducking her head. "Thanks for trying to understand."

"I don't want you to be in trouble, Daisy. I want to help you and Connor and make sure you're both safe."

"Yeah. Um, I'll see you later."

Daisy started to walk away.

"Daisy," Joy said, and she turned to face her again. "You take good care of Mr. Billingsly. He's depending on you."

"I will."

Joy watched her walk away, wondering if she had handled this the right way. Wondering if she should follow up on the little florist card and the notepad she had in her purse. If nothing else happened, maybe she would just leave them there. No, she ought to talk to Anne, Evelyn, and Shirley about what she had found out and what they ought to do next. Then she thought maybe she should talk to Anne and Evelyn about the party too. Tuesday would be here before they knew it, and she hadn't done much to prepare.

"Well," she told herself, "if I'm stuck on one problem, I might as well work on another one."

She looked up Revival's telephone number and gave them a call. The manager, a man named Chaz, told her they did an excellent buffet and that they had a private party room available for the twentieth. The price he quoted, though not cheap, was manageable. He was more than happy to make the reservation for her, but she told him she'd have to get back to him once she found out how many they would be expecting. Once she ended the call, she went down to records to talk to Evelyn.

There was nobody in sight at the records department, but after a few seconds of silence, Evelyn came out of the room they called the Vault. That was where they kept all the older hospital records and, as far as Joy could tell, it was a jumbled mess. Evelyn had a gleam of sweat on her upper lip, a lock of her silver hair hanging over one eye, and a stack of worn looking file folders in her arms.

"Joy," she breathed, and she dumped the folders on the counter with a huff. "What's up?"

"You look busy," Joy said. "Have I come at a bad time?"

"Right now, there's never a good time. We're trying to figure out some way to make the Vault a little more user friendly, but that's not going to happen anytime soon, and I need a break. Want to sit for a few minutes?"

"Sure. I was hoping we could talk."

Evelyn glanced around. "Are we alone?"

"I think so."

"Is this about the party?"

"Partly. I called Revival to check on what they had for larger parties. They have a private room and do buffets, but the price they quoted me was pretty hefty. Do you think we ought to try something else?"

"We might have to," Evelyn said. "I've had a few more people—"

Both of their phones buzzed right then, and they both checked their text messages. They had a joint message from Anne asking if a couple of Shirley's friends up on the fourth floor could come to the party.

"Hmm, do you have time for the three of us to talk for a minute?" Joy glanced at her watch. "If she's still at the hospital. She might already be gone."

"Maybe I'd better get back to work," Evelyn said. "We can have a conference call tonight, if you're up for it."

"Okay. Do you have time for a quick update on Connor Sherman?"

"Definitely. Did you get a chance to go to the florist?"

"I did." Joy brought out the card and the notepad Daisy had written on. "Your opinion?"

"They sure look the same. Is that Daisy's writing on the notepad?"

Joy nodded. "She didn't know why I asked her to write that until afterward. I think she was pretty shocked when I showed her the card."

"She must have been. What did she say?"

"She says she didn't send the flowers or write the card. I think I believe her." Joy hesitated for a moment. "Mostly."

"Mostly?"

"I don't know her that well. Apart from seeing her here at the hospital, I don't know her at all. She seems very sweet, and I'd rather not think that someone that young could do something underhanded like that."

"It's hard to tell sometimes. If someone is ambitious or desperate..."

"I don't know if she's desperate," Joy said, "but she does need to get a scholarship of some kind if she's going to go to college right after high school. Her family can't afford to do much for her in that respect."

"Is she likely to get a scholarship?"

"I think she has a good chance. She's probably going to be her school's salutatorian, but only because it looks like Connor will beat her and everybody else for valedictorian. She wouldn't be eligible for the scholarship the school offers, but that wouldn't really affect others she might apply for. Unless she thinks Connor having a lot of health problems will set him back a year, and that would be pretty extreme."

Evelyn frowned thoughtfully. "Maybe the money has nothing to do with it at all. Maybe she's simply tired of him being a step ahead of her all the time."

"Don't think I haven't wondered. I'm hoping, though, that it wasn't sent by her."

"But it couldn't be only an accident because some well-wisher didn't know Connor's allergic to daisies. The whole thing with the card, whether it was from Daisy or someone else, proves that there's something going on. Someone tried to make it look like she sent the flowers."

"Yes, I know, and I told her that, even though nothing serious happened, there would be an investigation if there was another incident. I think she's too smart to try this again when she knows she'd be the main suspect if anything else happens."

"I hope you're right. It sounds like Connor has enough on his plate without somebody trying to make him sick." Evelyn checked her watch again. "I'd better get back to the Vault. Are we having a conference call about the party tonight or what?"

"That'd be good if you're planning to be home."

"Yeah, I should be. Seven?"

"That ought to work. Let me text Anne and see."

Joy typed in a quick message and got a quick response.

7 TONIGHT OKAY.

"All right, we're on," Joy said. "By the way, have you ever heard of Swarna LeFrye?"

Evelyn looked puzzled. "Swarna? Is she from the Middle East?"

"I'm pretty sure she's American. She sounds like she's from California, though she's evidently traveled all over the world. She's very cosmopolitan. Very artsy. She's a filmmaker. She's been following Connor around since he was a baby, making a documentary about social development of extraordinarily smart children or something."

"That's interesting. How does Connor feel about it?"

Joy shrugged. "I think he's tired of it, to be honest. And he's got a doctor who's been studying his development as he matures. Something to do with how his intelligence affects the process. It's a Dr. Dahlman. Have you heard of him?"

"Dahlman? You're kidding me. Really?"

"Really. Do you know him?"

Evelyn laughed grimly. "He's the reason we've been scrambling the way we are. He asked Dr. Morton to authorize him to see some fairly old records. I don't know what the specifications are in particular, but the records are old enough that people can look at them without the patient's permission. Dr. Morton wants them for Dr. Dahlman's research."

"That's interesting. How far back?"

"Well, we can't release records until after fifty years, so no later than '72. I don't know what he'll get out of them, but he was very specific about which records he wanted. That is if we can find them."

"Good luck with that."

"Tell me about it. So this guy is studying Connor too. No wonder Connor wants out."

"Yeah, I get the idea that he doesn't want to be anything but a normal kid."

"Oh man," Evelyn said warily.

"What?"

"You don't think he could be doing this himself, do you? I mean, to get out from under all this."

"That's...something I hadn't thought about. I'll have to consider that possibility, but it doesn't seem like something he'd do. He wants out of the hospital, not to stay longer. At this point we don't have a lot to go on, but you know what I know so far, so keep your eyes open."

"Right. When I'm not buried in the Vault anyway."

"What about Shirley? Has she said anything to you about her birthday?"

"Just that she's looking forward to Tuesday night," Evelyn said. "As far as I can tell, she doesn't suspect anything."

"Good. Well, I'd better get going. We'll talk with Anne tonight. Are you keeping track of the people who have asked about Shirley's birthday?"

"I haven't made an official list, but I will before tonight. I'll add the people who I know would like to come too, if that's all right."

"Whatever you think. That'll give us a good idea of how many to plan for." Joy gave Evelyn a little wave. "Talk to you soon. Don't work too hard."

Evelyn huffed and then grinned and waved back. Then she returned to the Vault.

Joy stood where she was for a moment. She hadn't thought before about whether Connor might be sabotaging himself. He seemed determined to take charge of his life and stop being a lab rat, as he called it. It didn't seem at all likely that he would be behind everything that had been happening, but she certainly didn't know who was.

Chapter Eight

Joy walked home in the September sunshine. It was still warm—it usually was in Charleston this time of year—but she could tell the weather was at last turning toward fall. Cooler temperatures, even though they weren't here quite yet, would be a refreshing change from the summer's heat. Today there was a fresh wind off the ocean that rustled the palm trees and blew the rest of yesterday's storm clouds toward the horizon.

She crossed East Bay Street, glancing as always at the series of colorful houses that made up Rainbow Row. It was a view she never tired of, reminding her how much she loved living here in the middle of so much historic beauty.

The walk from work to home always refreshed her mind and gave her a chance to process the events of the day. As she turned onto the brick walkway that led to her two-story peninsula house, she again added to her mental to-do list. She, Evelyn, and Anne would have to talk about the financial aspect of the party, who would pay for what and what the limits would be. Before she dropped her purse on the little table by the door, she took out her cell phone and called Roger.

"Hey," he said when he picked up, and she could hear the sound of his car engine and the traffic noises around him. "How are you, Joy?"

"I'm fine. Do you have a few minutes to talk?"

"I'm on my way to a meeting with some of the hospital's major donors, but I'm about fifteen minutes away. So, yeah, if that counts as a few minutes, they're all yours. What's on your mind?"

Joy kicked off her shoes and made herself comfortable on the couch. "Since you're the fundraising expert, I thought I'd ask your opinion about Shirley's party."

"I thought we'd all chip in," he said. "No?"

"Well, that's what I thought too. Now it's gotten a little more complicated. Some of Shirley's friends at the hospital have asked if anybody's planning something for her. I don't know how many at this point, but I'm supposed to discuss it with Evelyn and Anne later on tonight. Sounds like there might be five or six more who'd like to come, and I'm thinking that it would be better if we did something a little more casual than Revival."

"A buffet?"

"I asked about that, and yes, they can do it. And having fifteen or twenty people would be all right if we got their party room, but is that the best way to go? What do you think?"

"You know Shirley a lot better than I do. What do you think she'd like?"

"I picked Revival in the first place because she really enjoyed it when she was there before, but that was when we were going to have four couples and nobody else. Now I'm wondering if we should go somewhere where people would feel more comfortable. And, to be honest, somewhere a little more affordable for everyone. I know a lot of people don't want to spend a lot of money on just a dinner out."

"You're right about that. The more people involved, the more you have to consider not being cost prohibitive."

"So maybe a party room at a less expensive place? Knowing Shirley, she'll be more interested in having her friends there than in what kind of food is served."

"That sounds reasonable to me," Roger said. "Are we still talking about Tuesday? And everyone being there waiting to surprise her?"

"Definitely."

"Then all you have to do is figure out who to invite and where to move the party."

"I'm going to talk to Evelyn and Anne about that. I think they both have a few names for our list."

"Good. I'll keep the evening open, and you tell me when and where when you've got it all ironed out."

"Perfect. I'll definitely keep you posted."

"Are we still on for tomorrow?" he asked over the roar of a nearby engine.

"That's what I'm planning on. Do we know what we're doing yet?"

"My sister was telling me about something she and her husband did a couple of weeks ago," Roger told her, "and they had a great time. What would you think about a walking food tour?"

"Um, I don't think I've ever heard of that. What is it exactly?"

"Emily told me they had a guide who took them to various places, telling them the history of where they were and describing the food traditions, and letting them taste whatever that place specialized in. She said most of the time they were in the French Quarter, in the original walled city of Charleston. They walked and ate for about two and a half hours."

"Wow," Joy said. "That's a long walk."

"She said it was wonderful. Even if you know Charleston, there's always something new to find out."

"I haven't been here long enough to say I know Charleston well yet, and I would love to find out more. She said the food was good?"

"They loved it. She said she and her husband were both stuffed by the end of the tour."

"What all did they have?"

"I don't remember everything she said," Roger admitted, "but all the traditional things, grits, benne wafers, seafood, collard greens, barbeque, gourmet chocolates. It was a pretty good variety. She said there were a lot of places they wanted to go back to so they could have an actual meal there."

"Mmm, you're making me hungry now."

"So is that a yes? It's a long walk."

"It's a definite yes," she told him.

"I was hoping you'd say that, because I went ahead and made us reservations."

"That's perfect. I'm surprised you could get us in at such short notice."

"Me too, but they had a cancellation, so I thought I'd better snap it up."

"I love the idea," Joy told him. "It's something I would never have thought of."

"I was looking for something that would be a little more interesting than merely a burger and a movie, so I'm glad you like it."

"I haven't had benne wafers since I moved here," Joy said.

The traditional sesame seed wafers had been brought from Africa in the seventeenth and eighteenth centuries and were long thought to bring good luck.

"We'll make sure we get some," Roger assured her.

She heard his car idle for a moment or two and then the motor surged. The light must have turned green.

"Are you almost at your meeting?" she asked.

"Nearly. I probably should hang up. But I'll see you tomorrow. You'd better get your walking shoes out."

"I walk to work and back every day," she told him. "I think I can handle this."

"Good. I'm looking forward to it." He was silent for a moment. "Looking forward to seeing you."

She felt a little flutter in her stomach. Yes, they were just friends at this point, but she couldn't help wondering if someday they might be more. He was definitely fun to be with, and it was so like him to pick something unusual for them to do tomorrow.

"Me too," she said. "And you'll have to tell me all about your donor meeting when you get a chance. You know the hospital always needs money."

"I do. And I think I can get these people to join me in helping out."

"I don't know how they would be able to resist."

He chuckled. "I'll let you know if your faith in me is justified."

"All right. Well, you made me hungry telling me about our walking tour, so I'm going to get me something to eat and then talk to Anne and Evelyn about the party. I'll text you any updates, okay?"

"That's fine."

She heard his car slow to a stop.

"I'm here now," he told her, "so I'd better go."

"Okay. Good luck with the donors."

"Thanks," he said. "Talk to you soon."

He disconnected, and she immediately looked up the walking tour he had told her about. It looked fabulous, and the reviews for it were great. She was eager to experience it for herself. Then, since it was really still a little early for dinner, she decided to look up Swarna LeFrye.

She typed in *swarna.com* and was taken to a page filled with stunning photographs. Many of them were of wildlife around the world. Many were of children, frequently in impoverished or even hazardous situations, but there were plenty that expressed the joy of childhood regardless of the nationality, wealth, or culture of the child in the picture.

She clicked on the FILMS tab, and found a long list of titles. She clicked on *The Branch* and found a description of the film along with Swarna's comments on making it. There was also a video link, so Joy clicked on it. It was fifteen seconds of a branch floating lazily down a stream in the dappled sunlight through the trees. Again the photography was stunning, but she wasn't sure she was up to watching seventy-seven minutes of it.

There were links to the button one and to the arson one too. Maybe she'd watch those samples later on. After she ate. After she talked to Anne and Evelyn. She did check out the "About Swarna" section of the website. Swarna had evidently been everywhere and had done everything, including going to Africa with a missionary group when she was in high school. It was curious though that there was nothing there about her family or her childhood or her education. It mentioned the awards she had won and that her permanent residence was in Charleston, but that was all.

Joy certainly didn't blame her for not wanting to post a lot of personal information for the world to see, but it would have been nice to find out more about her in general. On a whim, she tried Wikipedia. The article was mostly a rehash of her website, a description of her world travels and of her films. It even used the same photograph of Swarna that was on her website. Joy clicked on the photo and studied it for a moment. It was probably between five and ten years old, but Swarna had evidently not changed very much since it was taken. Except in the picture her nose wasn't pierced.

Joy clicked on the POETRY tab and found a number of poems, most of them without punctuation or capitalization, none of them rhyming. A few were thought-provoking, and some were confusing, but she was no expert on poetry anyway. A few of the authors Joy recognized, but many of the poems were credited to anonymous or to no one at all. None of them were Swarna's, but they all seemed to fit the theme of the website, adding something to the picture it painted of Swarna herself. Clearly her creative work was everything to her, but how far would she go to get the most dramatic story possible? What had happened to Connor lately was certainly more intriguing than him merely being in the hospital for knee surgery.

Next, Joy did a search for Dr. Eugene Dahlman. He didn't have a personal web page, but his name was mentioned on several professional sites. His credentials were good, and he was listed as having contributed to a number of scientific studies, most of them having to do with brain function and adaptation. But she couldn't find anything that he had done completely on his own. Evidently his work with Connor was his solo debut. The only biographical information she found on the doctor was a mention that he lived with his family in Charleston, South Carolina. Still, he was getting a lot of "bonus" information about Connor by being able to study his brain during these recent incidents. Was his research more important to him than the boy?

On a whim, Joy tried to see what she could find on Veronica Sherman and her family. She found an obituary for James Robbins Sherman showing he had left behind him a wife, Veronica, and two children, Hailey and Connor, as well as two sisters and a number of nieces and nephews. There was an article about Connor winning a mathematics competition when he was twelve and one about him and his sister organizing a group of students to clean up trash along I-26.

Veronica had her own page on social media, and Joy scrolled through that for a few minutes. The majority of what she posted was about her children, and most of that was about Connor. There were a few cute memes about child-rearing. A few recipes. Some family photos, including an especially cute one of Connor sound asleep in his baby swing and one of him with his hands and face full of icing from his first birthday cake. It had to be hard for Veronica, especially after losing her husband, but they seemed like a happy family. Of course, it was easy to pretend over the internet.

By the time Joy stopped her searches, it actually was dinnertime, and she realized she was hungry. She fixed herself a ham sandwich, and by the time she had eaten it and cleaned up after herself, it was time to talk to Anne and Shirley. At seven o'clock on the dot her phone rang. It was both of them.

A Genius Solution

"Here we are," Evelyn said when Joy answered the phone.

"Great. Have you thought about what we're going to do on Tuesday?"

"We have several names to add to the guest list," Anne replied.

"How many is several?" Joy asked her.

"Um, seven. I have seven anyway. How many do you have, Evelyn?"

"I have four," Evelyn said. "Actually five. Carol Anderson definitely wants to come if we have anything."

Joy got a pencil and paper from the table next to the couch and wrote down the names Evelyn and Anne had. "So the original four couples make eight. Regina and Dot make ten, and your five and Anne's seven makes another twelve. That's twenty-two. I'm thinking we ought to scrap the idea of going to Revival completely. We could still pick a nice place, but maybe something a little more affordable. What do you two think?"

"I agree," Evelyn said. "I don't think we ought to ask people to spend a lot merely to come to Shirley's party. We can have a sit-down meal still, but maybe something more modest."

"That sounds fine to me," Anne agreed. "The main thing is getting everybody together and making it a special evening for Shirley. She'll enjoy that more than anything else."

"And we can still have it be a surprise," Joy added. "All we need to do is make sure everybody we invite knows to keep the secret. Shirley doesn't know anything except we're going to pick her up, so everybody can be waiting for us at the restaurant."

"The question now," Anne said, "is where we're going to have it."

Joy considered for a moment. "Is there any place Shirley has mentioned in particular that she likes? Maybe somewhere she hasn't gone recently."

"Oh, wait," Evelyn said, "I remember. It was that place with crab-and-shrimp rice. The one over on Blake."

"Yeah," Anne said, "that little hole-in-the-wall-looking place. The orange building. Hannibal's."

"I don't think I'm familiar with that one," Joy admitted.

"We haven't been there in a while," Anne said. "Not since you've moved to Charleston. It's more of a laid-back place."

"Soul food," Evelyn told them. "Really good too."

"The place is kind of small," Anne said, "but it ought to be able to handle twenty-two of us."

"All right then." Joy wrote down the name of the restaurant. "I'll give them a call and see what they say, and if we can make a reservation. Do you think we're set as far as the number of people is concerned?"

"These are the ones who've asked specifically," Anne said. "There are more we could invite if you think we should. But we need to make some kind of decision soon. We're running out of time."

"True," Evelyn said. "Is there anyone in particular we should ask? I think our list has most of Shirley's friends, but there's always someone who gets missed."

"I could talk to the people on the list and see if they know of someone we shouldn't leave out," Joy offered.

"Within reason," Anne said. "Hannibal's isn't that big."

"You haven't told anyone we're actually planning anything yet, have you?" Joy asked.

"No," Evelyn said. "The ones I've talked to approached me, and I think it was the same for you, wasn't it, Anne?"

"Exactly. All I told them was that we'd let them know if there was going to be a gathering."

"All right," Joy said. "Let me contact Hannibal's and see what they say, and then I'll let you both know."

"Great," Anne said. "Well, I'd better get going. I'm supposed to help Addie make a poster about mammals for school while her mom's busy."

Joy chuckled. "Good luck."

"Well, she'll have to decide what she wants to do. I'm there mostly for moral support and to answer questions. And I'm sure I'm on cleanup duty too, once the masterpiece has been made."

"That sounds fun," Evelyn said. "I think I'm going to crash early. I've been hauling around files all day and breathing in enough dust to put a haunted house to shame."

"How's that going anyway?" Joy asked her. "What exactly is Dr. Morton asking you to find for Dr. Dahlman?"

"I don't exactly know. All we get is names and approximate dates. Then we go file diving. What the doctors do with the information later, I have no idea."

"Have you found out anything else about who might have sent Connor those daisies?" Anne asked. "Was it only a mix-up?"

"Oh, I need to bring you up-to-date," Joy said, and she told her what she had told Evelyn earlier about her talk with Daisy and how her handwriting looked very similar to the writing on the card that had come with Connor's flowers. "Like I told Evelyn, I don't think Daisy would do something like this, but I can't say I know that for sure."

"This might sound strange," Anne said after a pause, "but the way you describe Connor, it seems like he's tired of having to jump through a lot of extra hoops all the time. Do you think he could be sabotaging himself?"

Joy couldn't deny that she had speculated about the same thing since Evelyn had mentioned it.

"Anything's possible, I suppose," she said, "but I don't think so. He wants to go to college as soon as he can, and this is keeping him in the hospital instead. And it's making him just that much more interesting to the people studying him. I understand that he's been getting healthier and healthier as he's gotten older. He's only in the hospital because of his knee surgery. I don't see a reason for him doing this himself."

"You're probably right. And how would he have gotten a sample of Daisy's handwriting? Plus he would have had to order the flowers and get the card on them somehow. Did Daisy say it was on the flowers when she brought them up?"

"I can't remember, but I can ask her. I never actually told you about going to the florist, did I?"

"Oh yeah, I meant to ask you about that," Evelyn said.

"The clerk there said the daisies were ordered by a woman," Joy told her, "kind of nondescript, average, and that she had a scarf over her hair and was bundled up in a raincoat. So she could have been anyone."

Evelyn giggled. "Probably not Dr. Dahlman though."

"No, that full beard would have given him away." Joy laughed and then sobered. "I hadn't really thought of him. Actually, I haven't talked to him except for a couple of minutes the other day. I suppose he would like to keep Connor around for a while for all those tests."

A Genius Solution

"But is there anything that would tie him to those flowers or the card? And how would he have gotten a sample of Daisy's writing?"

"I don't know," Joy admitted. "I hope there won't be any more problems," Anne said. "It sounds like Connor has enough to deal with without having someone out to get him."

"I hope so too. I feel bad for him going through all this."

"Well, I'd really better go now," Anne said. "I still have to pick up Addie so we can get started on her project. She'll be waiting for me."

Evelyn exhaled. "I think I'm going to eat ice cream and watch old movies before I go to bed."

"You two have fun," Joy said. "I'll call Hannibal's and get back to you."

"See you tomorrow," Evelyn said.

"Talk to you then," Anne said, and they both hung up.

Joy put down her phone and scanned the list of names Anne and Evelyn had given her. Then she looked up the number for Hannibal's. Might as well find out what she could about what kind of accommodations they had for larger parties before she did anything else. She added a note to herself that she needed to talk to Dot about getting Shirley's mother to the party too, once the actual arrangements were finalized.

Before she picked up her phone again, she took the card from the florist and the sample of Daisy's handwriting out of her purse and studied them for a moment. Anne had said she hoped nothing else happened to Connor Sherman. Joy hoped so too, but she still didn't know how the incident with the flowers could possibly have been purely accidental. The note, forged or not, was proof of that.

Maybe Connor's reaction to the daisies had been more severe than expected and the sender would be too scared to make any other attempts. Or maybe the culprit knew that it wouldn't be easy to make another try now that Connor's mother was on high alert and that would end any further mischief. Or, and Joy was afraid this was the most likely possibility, maybe Connor was still in danger.

Joy sighed and put the party and the daisies and everything else from the hospital out of her mind. She was looking forward to spending tomorrow with Roger and forgetting about everything she had been stressing over for the past few days.

Still, she couldn't help wishing Dr. Morton had let Connor go home for the weekend. He'd be a lot safer there.

Chapter Nine

SATURDAY WAS PERFECT FOR THE walking tour. The weather was gorgeous, just a touch on the cool side but sunny and bright with a breeze that blew in fresh from the ocean.

Joy pushed away the plate containing what was left of her South Carolina barbeque. "That was delicious, but I'm stuffed. And we still have a lot more places to see."

"And things to eat," Roger said with a grin. "Are you having fun?"

"This has been amazing. Our guide knows so much about the city that I've never even heard of."

"That's the point of coming, I mean, besides the food. The history lessons have been fascinating."

"And they're right about getting an idea of what restaurants we'd like to come back to in the future. I've added several to my list."

"Good," Roger said. "That'll give us a lot of choices next time we go out."

There was that fluttery feeling in her stomach again. It would have been a perfect day if her party to-do list didn't keep popping into her head. She was running out of time, and nothing was really settled yet.

She'd have to get Evelyn and Anne on another conference call once she got home, but maybe she should just see to things herself.

They both had a lot to do, not just with work but with their husbands and families too. Joy didn't have anyone depending on her. Surely she could handle a birthday party on her own.

She had to decide what they were going to serve at the party and how it was going to be paid for. That was after she decided where the party was going to be in the first place. Then she had to figure out how people would be invited. It was too late for actual invitations. She'd invite each one personally. And she had to make sure that Dot knew where to bring Regina and when, but she couldn't do that until she'd decided on where and when.

First things first, she told herself. *I need to decide what we're going to do. Cake and punch? Cake and punch and appetizers? What kind of appetizers?*

She still liked the idea of Hannibal's, but she didn't know if they'd have a party room that would fit a lot of people. Best thing to do was call them up and see. And then—

"Anybody home?"

Joy blinked and felt her face turn warm seeing Roger looking at her inquiringly. She was glad to note a touch of humor in expression too.

"I'm sorry, Roger. I've got that party on my mind, and I meant to forget about it today. Forgive me?"

"I thought you had that all worked out. Is it off now?"

"What I told you about is off, yes. Now we have more people coming, and I think we're going to a place called Hannibal's."

"Hannibal's. Yeah, I've been there before. It's pretty casual, but the food is great. Does Shirley like it?"

"She does. And I can tell by looking at the menu that it's nothing like Revival, but fun doesn't have to be expensive, does it?"

"Of course not. Are you that stressed about it? Anything I can do?"

"No. I appreciate it, but I know you're a busy man. I'll be all right."

"I guess Evelyn and Anne are helping out."

She didn't say anything.

"Or did you decide they were too busy too?" he asked.

She sighed. "I know they'd do more if I asked, but really, they've got husbands and families to deal with besides their work. I don't have nearly as many responsibilities as they do, being on my own."

"Hold on a minute. I know you're single right now, but it's not like you're totally alone. You have a family too. I'm sure your daughter and your grandchildren need you as much as Anne's and Evelyn's families need them. You have a job as much as Evelyn does. I know Anne's busy as a volunteer and as the chaplain's wife too, but that doesn't mean you're not as busy as either of them. Have you discussed this with them at all?"

"Well, some," she admitted.

"And since you're single, you have to do everything around your place yourself. I don't see how that makes you less busy than your married friends."

Joy chuckled. "I definitely want their input on what we ought to do, but I thought I'd go ahead and set everything up so they wouldn't have to worry about it. They've got a lot to take care of right now."

"Like everybody, Joy. Including you. Shirley's their friend, isn't she? Isn't this party from all three of you?"

"Yes, of course."

"Then I can't see any reason they wouldn't be happy to help. I've seen all four of you together. You're family. You don't have to do all this by yourself."

"You're right." She laughed, feeling silly and relieved at once. "I think I've got it figured out anyway, but I do want to talk it over with them. If they agree about Hannibal's, I'll take care of the reservations and the menu. And maybe, since they're the ones who've been adding to the guest list, I'll ask them if they'll take care of inviting people."

"That doesn't sound like too much to ask," Roger said. "And what about the cake?"

Joy blew out her breath. "I need to find out what kind is Shirley's favorite and then find a great place to order a nice big one."

"I know a wonderful cake maker. He's done desserts for a lot of our functions, and I've never tasted anything he's made that wasn't delicious. Do you want me to get him to make something?"

"Hmm. I'm not sure. I guess it depends on how much money we're talking about."

"Sure. How were you planning to cover the cost of the party?"

"I need to talk to Evelyn and Anne about it, but I was thinking we'd split it three ways, our gift to Shirley. And we'd pay for the cake."

"That would be nice. How about this? Let me take care of the cake. That'll be my gift."

"Oh Roger, you don't have to do that. We can pay for it."

"And keep me from getting credit for the showiest part of the night? Not gonna happen."

She laughed. He was so sweet.

"Are you sure?" she asked. "If you've got some amazing cake designer, I'm sure that won't be cheap."

"And neither am I. You find out what kind she'd like and decide if you want it to look a special way, and I'll see to the rest. You won't have to think about it again."

"Oh, that would be wonderful. And I know she'll love it. I'll talk it over with Anne and Evelyn and let you know."

"Just don't wait too long to get back to me. Andre is usually very busy."

"He must be quite elite. Do you think it's already too late to get him in time for the party?"

"I think I can get him to do it. I send a lot of business his way, and he tries to be as accommodating as he can when I ask for a favor."

"I'll try to call you back about it tonight after I get ahold of the girls."

"And y'all think of something fun for the style of it too," Roger said. "One luncheon I went to to raise money for the zoo featured a cake in the shape of a two-foot-high giraffe in a tuxedo. It looked and tasted amazing."

"Andre made that?"

"He did. I'd love for Shirley to have something special. Something that lets her know what she means to you three and to all her friends."

"I'd like that too."

"All right. I'll take care of it."

"And thanks for the pep talk."

"You're more than welcome, Joy. Anytime." He glanced at his watch. "We're scheduled to be here for another fifteen minutes. Why don't you give Hannibal's a call and see what you can find out?"

"Are you sure you won't mind if I do it right now? Right in the middle of our tour?"

"We have time. Go ahead."

She took a pen and a piece of paper from her purse and then called the restaurant. It was early yet for Hannibal's, but she hit the jackpot when the man who answered the phone happened to be the manager.

He told her that, yes, they did have a party room for about thirty people. She told him the guest list was actually twenty-two. He quoted her a price for the room, drinks, and finger foods, and she told him she'd call back once she talked it over with her friends.

"What did they say?" Roger asked her once she hung up.

"They can do the food and the drinks and provide the room."

She told him the price.

"That seems very reasonable," he said. "What's on the menu?"

"That's for unlimited tea and lemonade, their special smoked neck bones and pigtails, and mini ham, turkey, and egg sandwiches for thirty. What do you think?"

"That sounds perfect to me."

"But what if it's nothing like Evelyn and Anne had in mind for the party? And what if Shirley would rather have dinner with the three of us and nobody else?"

"You can talk it over with them after the tour, right?"

"Right." Joy exhaled, smiling again. "I'll have to call them anyway and make sure they're okay with paying what the restaurant manager quoted me. Maybe I should find a less expensive place, though the prices actually seem very reasonable. Maybe—"

"I think it'll be fine," Roger said. "And I bet they'll tell you the same thing. Tell them about it this evening and ask them about the cake. If they're okay with everything, then you're pretty much set, aren't you?"

Joy nodded.

"What if I call Andre right now and see if he can work you in before Tuesday?"

"I still need to talk to Anne and Evelyn about what kind of cake we want."

"I can tell him that later. Right now I want to make sure he can do it in the first place."

To Joy it seemed like a minor miracle, but Roger assured her that Andre could indeed work Shirley's cake into his schedule.

"You're amazing," she told Roger once he ended the call.

"Andre's amazing, and that's one less thing you need to worry about today."

"Yes, it is. Thank you."

"Okay, then let's enjoy the rest of our tour and forget the party for now. What do you think?"

"I think that's the best idea I've heard all day."

Her mental to-do list tried to nudge her once again, but she pushed it firmly away. Tonight was soon enough to worry about it. For now she was eager to get to wherever they were serving those benne cakes.

"I wanted to tell you both what I found out about having the party at Hannibal's," Joy said once she got Anne and Evelyn on the phone that evening.

"Definitely," Anne said, "but you have to tell us at least a little about the walking tour."

"Did you have a good time?" Evelyn asked.

"We had a great time," Joy said. "I highly recommend it, and if you want some idea for good places to eat in town, let me know. I have quite a few new ones on my list. But for now we'd better talk about the party. We're running out of time here."

"True," Anne said. "What did you find out?"

Joy told them about Hannibal's.

"What do you think?" she asked them finally. "I want to make sure this is going to be something Shirley will love, so if this isn't it, let me know now. I'm open to suggestions."

"I think it's great," Anne said. "Fun and casual. People can come and go as they like."

"I'm glad we're including Regina too," Evelyn said.

"Oh, that reminds me," Joy said. "I've got to call Dot tonight and make sure she's on board. But here's the main thing. Well, two main things. I talked to Roger about a cake, which is not included in Hannibal's quote. What kind do you think Shirley would like best? I could name three or four, but this one ought to be special."

"Chocolate," Anne said.

"Definitely chocolate," Evelyn agreed. "As fudgy as possible."

"I was thinking that," Joy said, "but I know she loves angel food cake too."

"True, but since it's her birthday, the cake should be as decadent as possible."

"Ooh, yes," Anne said. "A really decadent chocolate cake would be perfect. But nothing added to the chocolate. She's not a fan of mint or mocha or anything like that. She wants her chocolate to actually be chocolate."

"I didn't tell you the best part," Joy added. "Roger knows a wonderful cake artist, and he'd like to get the guy to make Shirley's cake. And he's really an artist too, not just a baker, so Roger wants us to think of something creative for the design. Evidently the sky's pretty much the limit."

"Yeah, but can we afford that?" Anne asked dubiously.

"We don't have to. Roger said he'll cover the cost as his gift to Shirley."

"That's so sweet," Evelyn said. "You know, he's a real keeper."

"Evelyn," Joy said with exaggerated disapproval.

"Just sayin'."

"Anyway," Joy said deliberately, "he'll take care of that, and that leaves us to split the cost for Hannibal's for our part of the present. What do you two think? I didn't want to make a decision without clearing it with you both, and you won't hurt my feelings if you'd rather go a different direction."

"I say we should go for it," Anne said. "I've been trying to figure out what to get Shirley, and I couldn't find anything I thought she'd really love, but I'm sure she will love this."

"I think so too," Evelyn said. "I think you've done a great job, Joy, working this all out and making it something we can afford to do."

"I'm glad we're all on the same page on this then," Joy said. "As soon as we get off the phone, I'll call Hannibal's and make the arrangements. Then I'll call Roger and tell him we want a chocolate cake for the party. And I'll call Dot. But I do have a job for the two of you, if you don't mind."

"Fire away," Evelyn said.

"You've both given me names of people who've said they want to come to the party. Would you please go ahead and invite them for Tuesday night? I'm going to tell Hannibal's we're starting at seven, all right?"

"Perfect," Anne said. "And we'll make sure everybody knows mum's the word."

"Exactly," Joy told her. "Thanks for taking that off my plate. Now all we have to do is figure out what this wonderful cake should look like, and then I'll take care of the reservations."

"It would be great to have the cake reflect something that Shirley really likes," Evelyn considered. "Something outside of her job."

"That's the problem," Anne said. "Shirley's so busy working and taking care of her mom and having a little time to go out with Garrison, I don't think she really has any hobbies. She likes jazz, but she likes a lot of different kinds of music. Same for books and movies."

"That's true," Joy said. "I think she enjoys her friends more than some specific activity. And, yes, nursing is very important to her too. It's part of who she is. I wonder if there's a way we can reflect that."

They discussed the problem for a few minutes, offering and discarding a number of ideas. Then, almost simultaneously, they settled on one they thought Shirley would love.

"That will be perfect," Anne said.

"I agree," Evelyn added. "But what will it look like?"

"That's something we'll have to wait and see once Roger gets it from his cake-artist friend and brings it to the party," Joy said. "I'll tell him about it right away."

"Good," Anne said. "That'll be something else off your plate."

"Exactly. I'd better call Hannibal's and then call Roger and then call Dot. And you two had better get busy with the invitations. Tuesday is coming."

Chapter Ten

Monday morning, Joy walked to work feeling refreshed after her weekend with Roger and getting the party plans finalized. Time flew by, and that afternoon, once Lacy came in to work at the gift shop, Joy decided to take a few minutes to go around to talk to the people Anne and Evelyn had mentioned to her as wanting to know about a party for Shirley. They were all enthusiastic about coming to Hannibal's the next night and gave her the names of several more of Shirley's friends who might want to attend.

Joy talked to those people too, telling them the plan and that this was strictly top secret. The list of potential guests went from twenty-two to thirty-seven, and Joy called the manager of Hannibal's to let him know. She also told him that she didn't think all the guests would be at the party for the whole evening. She got him to agree that, if she and her guests didn't mind it being a little bit crowded, he could probably make it work for up to forty if necessary.

According to Ralph, Anne had already left for the day, so Joy went to the records department to talk to Evelyn. This time she found her already at her desk, but she was surprised to see who was there with her.

"Dr. Dahlman," Joy said, extending her hand. "How are you? I didn't think I'd see you here."

The doctor briefly wrapped his large hand around hers, his dark eyes twinkling behind his glasses. "It's good to see you again, Joy. Dr. Morton had an emergency to see to, so I thought I'd pop down here myself and check if I could get Evelyn to help me directly."

"Hi, Evelyn," Joy said. "Looks like you're busier than ever."

"They keep me hopping," Evelyn said with a smile. "If you'll excuse me, Doctor, I'll get the rest of the files you're asking for and be right back."

Dr. Dahlman nodded. "Thank you."

"Doing research?" Joy asked as Evelyn went into the Vault.

"Exactly," the doctor said. "As you know, I've been studying Connor Sherman for some time now, and I'm trying to find out if some of these patients had experienced any of the same issues he has and, since these are all older cases, if there's any information about what happened to them in their later years. I'm actually hoping that a few of them might still be alive and willing to talk to me about their experiences in adulthood. It would give me an idea if what I'm hypothesizing might actually be correct."

"That would be interesting," Joy said. "Is there something in particular they have in common?"

"It's been rather hit-or-miss," Dr. Dahlman said ruefully, "but I've found a few that might be exactly what I need. I'm trying to determine if there is any kind of connection between high intelligence and increased sensitivity to environmental factors."

"Environmental factors?" Joy made sure her expression didn't change. "Do you mean like allergens?"

"Exactly that," the doctor said. "It's been part of my study for some time now, and Connor's little incident gives me the perfect opportunity to collect more data on him and compare it to these other patients."

"I suppose Connor didn't care much for having to stay the whole weekend."

"Not much, though Dr. Morton hasn't released him to go home yet anyway. Connor's generally good-natured about all this, being a lab rat as he calls it, but I know he wants out. I think, more than simply not enjoying the testing itself, he wants to be treated like an average kid. And really, that's what he is. The intelligence doesn't keep him from wanting to do what other boys his age do or from wanting to be accepted and liked or from wanting to be seen as strong rather than weak. It's not easy being the different one."

"I suppose not," Joy said. "I'm impressed by how well he manages through all this. He seems like a typical kid to me. I mean, except for all the testing and the documentary made about him and that sort of thing."

"There's that," Dr. Dahlman said, his mouth turning up slightly under his mustache. "But I suppose I won't have him much longer. I have a feeling, though, that he won't vanish into anonymity once he gets out into the world. Besides intelligence, he has a very inquisitive mind and the ability to stick with a task as long as it takes in order to get it done. That, my dear, is practical genius. That young man will be going places, mark my words."

Joy couldn't help wondering if Dr. Dahlman perhaps expected to claim some credit in the future when Connor did whatever great things the doctor seemed to be predicting.

"It must be very difficult to work on a project like this over so many years," she said. "Are you also in practice? That must keep you pretty busy."

"Actually, I don't have private patients anymore. My study is funded by a government grant. No doubt some bureaucrat somewhere sees a potential policy maker in young Connor, but I don't think that's where the boy's interests lie. I think he's more likely to come up with the next big discovery that will affect the whole world. And yes, I certainly want to see what that is."

It was almost as if he had read her mind.

"And when Connor goes to college?" Joy asked him.

"I hope that won't be for a while yet. Not until the end of the school year at least. Longer if I can get his mother to agree. I think for his emotional well-being, because he really is very young despite being as mature for his age as he is, he should stay with his mother a bit longer. But that hasn't been decided yet."

"I'm curious. What will you do when he goes to college?"

"As I've said, I would try to stay in touch with him. I'd like to continue whatever testing I can as often as he would allow it. But there's not much I can do without his cooperation and his mother's consent."

"Does he have a lot of friends here?" Joy asked. "At his school?"

"He's not a loner, if that's what you're asking. School can be awkward for him at times because of the age difference between him and his classmates, but he has friends."

"Has he ever mentioned Daisy Graham to you? I think she has a number of classes with him."

"You mean the young woman who volunteers up here at the hospital," Dr. Dahlman said, nodding. "Yes, I've seen her a time or two."

"But has Connor ever said anything to you about her?"

"When I heard she was a schoolmate of his, I asked him about her. He seemed…hesitant to say much, bad or good. He would only acknowledge that she was in his class and say that she was 'okay.'"

Was there some history between the two teens that neither of them was willing to admit? Perhaps another reason why Daisy would want to do something to spite Connor after all? It still seemed out of character for Daisy, but Joy couldn't dismiss the thought until she had some proof of Daisy's innocence.

"Do you think Connor will go home today? Maybe he's already gone."

"Actually, he and I just got through for the day, so I assume he's back in his room. I'm sure that if Dr. Morton was available, he'd send Connor home. I don't think it will be very long before he's released."

"I'd better go visit him while I can then," Joy said, just as Evelyn came back with a stack of files in her arms. "I'm going to see if Connor's still in his room, Evelyn. I'll catch up with you later. Dr. Dahlman, I hope you find what you need."

"Thanks," the doctor said.

"See you later," Evelyn added. "Call me."

"Okay."

Joy went to the second floor and found Connor sitting up in bed and Swarna in a chair beside him. They were laughing about something.

"Hi," Joy said as she came into the room. "It sounds like you must have had good news, Connor."

He shrugged, still smiling. "Hi. Yeah, I think so."

"Connor has an opportunity to visit MIT to see if that might be where he wants to go to school," Swarna said proudly. "Evidently someone's been talking him up."

"Wow," Joy said. "I'm impressed. That sounds like the perfect school for you."

"It would be great," Connor admitted. "If I make sure to get the Lackland Scholarship or something. What Mom and Dad put away for me might not be enough for MIT."

"Do you know who recommended you?"

Connor shook his head. "Not a clue. Are you sure it wasn't you, Swarna?"

Swarna smirked. "I'm the one who wants you to stick around a while longer, remember?"

"Yeah, yeah. Mom's going to have a fit though. I don't think she'd be able to handle it even if I went to Trident Technical here in Charleston."

"Massachusetts is pretty far," Joy said. "But maybe if you tell your mother you're finishing out the school year here, she would be more open to your going later."

"I don't know," Connor said, sagging a little against his pillows. "I've been bored at school for the past three years. There's a lot I want to do."

"Are you sure you're ready to live on your own? Even if it is in a dorm? That's a big step at your age."

"I think Mom's planning on moving close to whatever school I decide to go to. Even if I live on campus, she'll still be around. Hailey's already moved out. I will sooner or later. Mom's got to adjust. I figure this would be a good way to kind of ease her into it."

"I'm sure she'll miss you, no matter when you leave," Joy said.

Swarna nodded. "He's been taking care of his mother since his father died."

"I'm not abandoning her, you know," Connor said. "It's not like I'm never going to see her again once I leave home. But I need to be on my own too. I want to be able to go to school and not have someone worry about me being too tired or reading too much or looking too pale." He winced slightly. "Mom's a great mom, don't get me wrong, but she thinks I'm a baby still, and everybody thinks I'm a big mama's boy."

"At school?" Joy asked.

"Yeah. She insisted on sitting in on my third-grade class for a whole month just because one of the kids brought peanut butter cookies once. The teacher didn't even let us have them. After that, Mom would have the school nurse check on me all the time. She wouldn't let me ride the bus. She always had to discuss whatever activities I could and couldn't participate in with the PE teachers. It was embarrassing."

"Is it still that way?"

Connor's tense expression relaxed. "Nah. We talked about it some, and she's backed off. But I know she still wants to hover. She needs to know that I'm nearly grown up. I'll be able to drive in a couple of months, and then she's going to be really nervous."

"It can be hard letting go of a child," Joy said. "But it can be very rewarding too."

"I don't want to hurt her feelings. I only want her to understand."

"You two will work it out, I'm sure. Where is she today?"

"She went to get some things for my sister's birthday next week. Hailey's coming home for the weekend, and Mom's really excited."

"She was here earlier," Swarna said. "Right before Connor went to do more tests with Dr. Dahlman." She glanced over at the slim white box on Connor's bed table. "It looks like you still haven't had a piece. I probably should take them back and eat them myself."

"Hey." Connor grabbed the box and clutched it to his chest. "You know I couldn't eat before I had bloodwork and stuff done. But I can now." He lifted the top off the box. "I was hoping it was chocolate buttercreams. Thanks!"

"Dark chocolate," Swarna said. "Your favorite."

"Sounds like you know what Connor likes," Joy said.

"Oh, we've gotten to know each other over the years. I've learned to be careful about what I give him to eat. No eggs, peanuts, shellfish, or soy."

"Fun, isn't it?" Connor said glumly.

"Better than a reaction," Swarna said. "I have allergies myself. Not quite as bad, but bad enough. We have to stick together, right, Connor?"

"Yeah."

"Have you been at the hospital the whole time?" Joy asked Swarna. "Or did you come back just to make sure Connor had his chocolates?"

"Actually, I had just gotten here when Dr. Dahlman came to take Connor away. Veronica and I talked for a little while, and then she went to run her errands. She told me that Dr. Morton was tied up on some emergency, so she couldn't ask him about whether Connor could be released today. I told her I'd see what I could find out, so I checked around a little. Dr. Morton came in a while after that and was good enough to let me ask some questions about how Connor's doing." She smiled at Connor. "Which he told me was wonderful."

"Please tell Mom that," he grumbled.

"I think too," Swarna went on, "that I've nearly gotten him convinced that he ought to do an on-camera interview for my film. Dr. Dahlman is really more about research and seeing if he can validate his theories about the maturation process of the highly intelligent brain. Dr. Morton is more involved in Connor's physical health and well-being. By the way, Connor, he said he's going to come talk to you and your mom when he gets a chance."

"Did he say I can go home now?"

"Not to me. He'll have to be the bearer of the good news, if there is any."

Connor grinned. "I'll take it however I can get it. I am so ready to go home." He offered her the box of candy. "Would you like one?"

"You don't have to ask me twice." Swarna popped a chocolate into her mouth and then closed her eyes. "Mmmmm. You know, there's a reason I bring you my favorite candy."

"Yeah. Um, would you like one?"

Connor took a piece for himself and then offered the box to Joy, and she took one too. The chocolate quickly melted in her mouth.

"Oh, these are heavenly. I'm going to have to get some of these for myself."

"I get them from this place on Priestly, off Riverland Drive," Swarna said. "Their chocolates are always so fresh."

"They must make them themselves."

"I believe they do."

"Thank you for sharing, Connor," Joy said. "I have to get back to work, but I'm glad I stopped by. It's great you might get to go home tonight instead of tomorrow too. How did things go with Dr. Dahlman?"

"Oh, same as always. Lots of questions, lots of puzzles to work, lots of scans and graphs, bloodwork, and I don't care what else. I want to get back to school, and I want to start talking to some of the colleges I'm interested in. I wish Mom would let me go ahead and enroll."

"Maybe you could take some online college courses to start with," Swarna suggested. "Then you would be able to start your classes without having to leave home."

"Yeah, I know. Mom and I talked about that. I think I probably will, at least until Christmas or something. I—" Connor coughed. "Sorry. I really would like to—"

He coughed again, harder now, and then drew a wheezing breath.

"Connor?" Joy said, moving closer to him. "Are you all right?"

"Yeah, I just—" He coughed again, his face reddening alarmingly. "Something's wrong."

Swarna struggled to breathe too, and her face turned dark under her tan.

Joy pushed the call button for the nurse and then she ran out to the nurses' station.

"Get a doctor in Connor Sherman's room. Now!"

Chapter Eleven

Joy was waiting in the hallway when Veronica approached Connor's room.

"Joy. I didn't expect to see you here. Do you want to hear some great news? I talked to Dr. Morton a little while ago. He says Connor can go home today."

Joy winced. "Something came up. Didn't the nurse call you?"

"No, but I noticed earlier that my phone battery was low. It's probably totally out." Veronica glanced toward the closed door. "What's wrong? Where's Connor?"

She tried to go into the room, but Joy stopped her.

"He's okay. He's fine. He's asleep right now."

"Let me see him."

"You can see him. He's all right. I told Dr. Morton I'd wait for you here and tell you what happened, but he wanted you to stay calm. Connor is fine. Really."

Veronica pressed her trembling lips together. "Okay. Okay. I'm calm. I want to see him."

"The doctor says he needs to rest, so please try to not wake him up."

"All right. Maybe you'd better tell me what happened out here. I don't want our voices to disturb him."

"First, he really is doing fine now. He had an allergic reaction to that candy Swarna brought."

"The candy? The chocolates she brought him earlier?" Veronica shook her head. "How can that be? She's brought him those a dozen times at least. They don't have anything in them that he's sensitive to. She's very careful about it."

"Something must have gone wrong this time. Swarna had a reaction too. She had to be rushed to the ER."

"Oh no. How is she?"

"She went home a little while ago. She's fine. But she's as baffled as we are. She says she bought the candy from the same place she always goes to. Dr. Morton took it to have it analyzed. He's afraid Connor might have developed a new allergy, though he says that's pretty unusual."

Veronica laughed faintly. "If it's unusual, Connor's the one who's likely to get it. Oh, I need to see him."

She pushed open the door. Connor was sprawled out on the bed, fast asleep. He looked very young.

"Poor baby," Veronica whispered, barely touching the lock of dark hair that had fallen over his forehead, and then she sank into the chair beside his bed. "What is going on? Why is someone doing this?"

Joy put her fingers to her lips. "Why don't we go back outside? He's doing all right, and the nurse's station is monitoring him."

Veronica looked longingly at her son for a moment more, and then she got up and walked out into the hall. Joy followed her into the nearby waiting room.

"Tell me what happened," Veronica said as soon as they sat down. "I suppose you've been away from the gift shop too long as it is."

"It's all right. I called the volunteer who helps me out part time. She can handle it." Joy poured some coffee into a Styrofoam cup and handed it to her. "Drink that and take a minute to calm down. I'll tell you what I know."

Once she had poured herself some coffee, Joy sat down next to Veronica.

"I don't understand," Veronica said after a tense moment. "Am I supposed to think this is only another accident?"

"I don't know. Swarna was with Connor when I came into the room. She had just been talking to Dr. Morton. We talked for a few minutes about Connor's school, and then he opened the box of candy. It must have been for the first time, because it was still full."

"Yes. Swarna brought it earlier, but Connor couldn't eat any because he was about to have bloodwork done."

"That's what he told me too. Connor was talking about wanting to get on with college and maybe taking some online courses while he's still finishing up high school. After a few minutes, he started coughing and having trouble breathing. I realized that Swarna was struggling too, so I called the nurse. They took Swarna to the ER, and Dr. Morton came and tended Connor in his room."

"Thank goodness. I need to talk to him."

"He said you can call him anytime, but he wants you to know that he's sure Connor will be fine. He wants him to stay in the hospital though."

"Of course. Did the doctor have any idea what might have set off the reaction?"

"I didn't see Swarna after they took her to the emergency room, so I didn't get a chance to ask her about it, but she said that she has some allergies too."

"Yes. I think that's partly why she's always been so careful about what she gives Connor."

"Whatever was in the chocolates must have been something they were both allergic to. I'm trying to figure out who would have had a chance to tamper with them."

"I knew I shouldn't have gone out," Veronica said fretfully. "I should have been here to make sure nobody tried anything."

"Is that something you usually do? Guard his food?"

"Well, no, but this time I should have."

"You couldn't have known," Joy told her. "So you and Swarna went to find Dr. Morton, right?"

"Yes. They told me earlier that he had been called to an emergency, but she wanted to talk to him about doing an interview for her film. I don't know if he agreed or not, since he didn't mention it when I called him a little while ago, and he told me Connor was fine to leave today."

"And you didn't come back to Connor's room from the time Swarna left the chocolates until now?"

"I did my errands and then called the doctor. Then I came straight here."

"And Swarna went to talk to Dr. Morton after she left the chocolates. Did she mention going anywhere else?"

"No. She must have spent the whole time talking to Dr. Morton. She can be very persuasive when she wants to be, and I know she wanted to talk to him about the interview she wants to do with him. She probably convinced him to do it."

"She mentioned that she thinks she almost has," Joy said. "That surprises me."

"Me too. He usually doesn't seem to have much patience for Dr. Dahlman or Swarna. He wants to take care of Connor without all the extra drama, he says. He calls it Connor's circus."

"So he and Swarna were still talking when you left them. And she and Connor were back in his room when I got there."

"I suppose neither of them would have seen anybody go into or come out of the room." Veronica looked toward the nurses' station. "What about whoever was on duty?"

"Nobody noticed anyone in particular. The man in the room two doors down from Connor's has a very big family, lots of children and grandchildren and their spouses and their children, and they've all been in and out. The nurses don't know who belongs where unless someone stops to talk to them."

"I simply can't think that this is a coincidence, Joy. Not after what happened with the flowers."

"I admit it would be unusual, but it's possible. Do you want to get the police involved?"

Veronica picked a little piece of Styrofoam off the rim of her cup. "I don't know. Would they even take me seriously? Connor has a history of medical problems, including various allergic reactions. Would they be able to prove someone was deliberately doing something?"

"They might be able to set your mind at ease by ruling it out."

"I thought you were going to do that. Did you find anything that would help?"

Joy thought of the florist's card she still had in her purse. Even if Daisy had been the one to send Connor those daisies to purposely cause him problems, surely she wouldn't have been so foolish as to try something else so soon. Not when she knew the writing on that card was so much like her own. Joy would have to talk to her again. She hoped Daisy would have an alibi for the time that box of candy had been left in Connor's room unattended.

"No, I'm sorry to say," she told Veronica. "Things didn't work out the way I thought they might, so I'm still right where I was before. Is it okay if I hang on to the card for a while anyway? I have some other ideas about what to do."

"Sure. Of course, the police will have to see it if we end up calling them in."

"You can call them any time. I'm not saying you shouldn't."

Veronica blinked hard, clearly trying not to cry. "I really don't know." She took a deep, steadying breath. "I think we ought to see what Dr. Morton has to say about the analysis. If it seems like somebody did this deliberately, then I'm calling the police. I can't let anything else happen to Connor."

"Of course not." Joy paused for a moment. "Veronica?"

Veronica looked at her questioningly.

"I don't want to put ideas into your head, but can you think of anybody who would put something in that candy so Connor would be sick, at least temporarily?"

Veronica's expression hardened. "You mean Daisy Graham?"

"Actually, I wasn't thinking about her. I haven't seen her around anywhere. I don't know if she's even in the hospital today."

"I haven't seen her lately, but that doesn't mean she isn't here. Who's in charge of volunteers anyway?"

"What if I check today's sign-in sheet? That could help us know pretty quickly whether or not she could have tampered with the chocolates."

"Okay. Yes, that would be good. But you know she could have come up here even if she wasn't scheduled to work."

"I know."

Joy thought again of the florist's card with what looked like Daisy's writing on it. If the chocolates had been tampered with and Daisy couldn't account for her whereabouts during the time Connor was out of his room, then Joy would have to tell Veronica, and probably the police, about how similar the two writing samples were. It made her feel a little bit sick to think of reporting Daisy, but as Veronica had said, they couldn't let anything else happen to Connor.

"But I was wondering if you had considered whether anybody else might be trying to keep Connor from leaving the hospital right now," Joy said. "For whatever reason."

"The only one I can think of is Daisy. She wants to go to Clemson, from what Connor tells me, and he's talked about that too. And about MIT. In Massachusetts."

"Evidently someone mentioned Connor, and they're interested in talking to him. He and Swarna were talking about it when I came into Connor's room, so maybe she was the one who recommended him. I don't know how he found out. Everything happened so quickly after that."

"But Massachusetts is so far away."

"I'm sure you and he will figure out what would be best for him to do," Joy said, "but for now, we really need to make sure he's protected. Do you think anyone else might be trying to make him sick or keep him in the hospital? Does anyone you know have a grudge against him?"

"I don't think so. Why in the world would anyone want to hurt him?"

"Maybe this person doesn't really want to hurt him per se, just slow him down a little. Dr. Dahlman and Swarna have both said they aren't through with their work with him."

"Well, yes, but that doesn't mean they'd do anything underhanded like this, does it? I mean, Dr. Dahlman is a doctor. He took the Hippocratic oath and everything. And Swarna, she loves Connor. She wouldn't hurt him."

"I hope not. I hope neither of them would, but we have to consider all the possibilities, don't we?"

"It sounds like Swarna did have a pretty bad reaction to the candy," Veronica said. "I suppose that rules her out."

"Not necessarily. She brought the chocolates, so it would have been easy for her to put something in them ahead of time. Then again, the box was left in Connor's room while he was gone, so anyone could have come in and doctored the chocolates."

Veronica's expression was grim. "Who do you think it could be?"

"Dr. Dahlman was with Connor the whole time he was out of his room, so he couldn't have tampered with the candy."

"Unless he had someone do it for him. Oh, but it couldn't be him. It couldn't."

"Is there anyone else you can think of?" Joy asked. "Anybody at all?"

"I just don't know. I can hardly think with everything that's going on. I mean, Massachusetts? Really? And maybe this was nothing more than a new sensitivity for Connor, and nobody's to blame."

Veronica looked at Joy almost pleadingly, and Joy reluctantly nodded.

"I suppose we ought to wait and see what Dr. Morton finds out from the analysis before we start blaming anyone."

She still didn't know how that florist's card could indicate anything but intentional mischief, whether or not Daisy was the actual mischief maker. Before she could say anything more, one of the nurses came into the waiting room.

"Mrs. Sherman? Dr. Morton just called. He said he's on the way and would like you to wait for him, if you don't mind."

"Oh yes," Veronica said. "Yes, of course."

"He should be here in just a minute."

"Thank you."

"Do you want me to leave you and Dr. Morton alone?" Joy asked as soon as the nurse left the room. "I would certainly understand."

"Oh no." Veronica clasped her arm. "Please don't go. You've been so helpful this whole time, and I'm so flustered right now, I might not remember everything the doctor has to say the minute after he's said it."

Joy patted her hand. "If you're sure you don't mind. I would like to hear what he has to say about the candy. And I do want to help. I don't want anything else to happen to Connor. What's already happened is enough."

"I wish I could take him home right now," Veronica said, her lips trembling. "He would be so much safer there. But I know Dr. Morton is going to want to keep him here for another night. I'm grateful that Connor's being taken care of, but I think we'd both be happier at home."

"You'll have to be extra careful from now on. Make sure Connor doesn't come in contact with anything you're not sure of."

"Maybe I ought to tell the police about this right now. They could have someone stand guard over Connor, couldn't they?"

"I'm not exactly sure what they'd do. Maybe while he's in the hospital, I suppose, but let's see what Dr. Morton says about the candy. Then you can decide what you want to do."

"Okay." Veronica glanced at the clock on the waiting room wall. "I wish he'd get here. I really ought to get back to Connor." She caught a quick breath. "Maybe we should have stayed outside his room and kept watch."

"No, everything is okay." Joy nodded toward the large windows that looked out onto the corridor and across to the door of Connor's room. "I've been watching while we've been in here. There was one visitor who walked down the hall, and a couple of nurses went toward the nurses' station. That was all. Nobody has gone into his room. Do you want to go check on him before Dr. Morton gets here?"

Veronica got up quickly. "I think I ought to. I'll make sure not to wake him."

Joy watched through the windows as she went across the hall and into the room. A moment or two later she came back looking a little calmer than before.

"He's still fast asleep, but he doesn't look quite so pale as before."

"He'll be all right," Joy assured her. "And we're going to make sure he stays that way." She looked out into the corridor and saw Dr. Morton coming toward the waiting room. "He's here."

"Oh." Veronica sniffled and then smoothed her hair back. "Do I look too awful?"

"You look fine. And Dr. Morton knows you've been through a lot today. Just try to relax."

"Mrs. Sherman," Dr. Morton said, reaching out to shake Veronica's hand.

"Hello, Doctor. Thank you for taking such good care of Connor. I feel so bad for not being here when he was having problems."

"He's going to be fine." The doctor put his hands on her shoulders and looked her steadily in the eye. "I promise." He pulled up a chair in front of the ones Joy and Veronica were sitting in and sat down. "Hello, Joy. Thanks for staying around until Veronica got here."

"I was happy to help."

"You've been a good neighbor."

He looked for a moment at Veronica as if he was waiting for her to let him know whether he ought to talk in front of Joy. Joy decided to give her a gracious way out in case she had changed her mind about having Joy stay.

"I'll be glad to let the two of you talk alone now, Veronica, if you'd like."

"No," Veronica said at once. "Please stay. Joy's been such a big help, Dr. Morton. You don't mind if she hears what you have to say, do you?"

"Not at all. That's totally your decision to make."

A Genius Solution

"Good, because I want her here. What did you find out about the chocolates? Has Connor picked up a new allergy?"

"No," Dr. Morton said, "but he has reacted to a very old one. Peanut oil."

"What?" Veronica's forehead puckered. "Those chocolates don't have peanut oil in them. Connor's eaten those since he was a little boy and never had a reaction. Swarna eats them too, and she's very allergic to peanuts."

"The label on the box doesn't list any peanut products," he explained, "but there was peanut oil in the candies all the same."

"So it was added to them when they were being made?" Joy asked.

"That seems unlikely. From what I can tell, a small amount of the oil was injected into each piece. Obviously, it was enough to cause a strong reaction in Connor and in Swarna."

"I thought that was sort of an interesting flavor for a chocolate buttercream," Joy said, thinking back on the piece she'd eaten. "But I barely tasted it. I don't know if I would have thought anything of it if I didn't know the chocolates had been tampered with."

"Unfortunately, it doesn't take very much of anything peanut related for Connor to have a reaction," Dr. Morton said. "I'm glad, though, that it was such a small amount."

"But there was nothing accidental about it," Veronica said solemnly.

"No. I don't think it could have been. I've written up a report of my findings, and I'm happy to give that to the police along with a statement."

Veronica sighed. "I didn't want to have to involve them, but I think it's time. I can't risk anything more serious happening to Connor."

"I know a detective, Rebekah Osborne," Joy said. "Do you want me to talk to her about this? I'm sure she'll come out and investigate."

"I'd appreciate it. I've never had to talk to the police about anything before."

"They're here to help. Hopefully, Rebekah will get to the bottom of this and catch whoever is behind it."

"I hope that doesn't mean you're going to stop investigating."

"I still have a few questions I want to ask," Joy said. "And I'll share with Rebekah whatever I find out too. She's much better at this than I am."

Veronica clasped her hands together in her lap. "I want to know exactly who's responsible."

Dr. Morton stood up, his mouth in a tight line. "Joy, you tell Detective Osborne to come see me. I'll give her all the information I can."

"Before you go, Doctor," Joy said, "can you tell me about your talk with Swarna LeFrye earlier?"

"There's not much to say. We talked about Connor. She wants to interview me for her film."

"Are you going to let her?"

Dr. Morton chuckled. "I'll admit I'm considering it. But I don't know when I'll have time for it. Anyway, I told her to write up her questions and give them to me so I can prepare what I want to say ahead of time. Then maybe I won't look like a buffoon on camera."

"I don't think that's possible," Joy said warmly. "But it is nice to be prepared. How long did you and she talk?"

"Hmm, I think she tracked me down in my office at about one fifteen or so, maybe one twenty, and she must have stayed about half an hour talking about filming Connor and some of her other projects. Forty minutes maybe. I know I had to leave for a meeting at two, and she was headed back to Connor's room."

"That fits," Joy said. "I went up to Connor's room a little after two, and she was there chatting with him. But anyone else could have come into the room while Connor was with Dr. Dahlman."

"True. Well, I'd better get back to work. Mrs. Sherman, you make sure Connor doesn't come into contact with anything you don't know about, all right? Or anybody."

"Yes, Doctor. Thank you."

He gave Veronica a comforting pat on the shoulder. "It's going to be all right. We'll just take extra good care of Connor for now."

Veronica relaxed a little bit. "Yes, we will."

"Joy," Dr. Morton said, "I'll see you later. Thanks for helping out."

"Anytime, Doctor."

"I'll see you both later."

"Joy," Veronica said when he was gone, "I meant what I said. I don't want anybody to get into real trouble. If it *is* Daisy...well, she's still very young. I don't want her life ruined."

"When I talked to her before, I was really convinced that either she was innocent or that she understood the gravity of what she had done with the flowers and that she wouldn't do anything like that again. We'll have to tell Rebekah about what happened earlier and let her follow up on it."

Joy knew that she would have to show the police that florist's card and the sample of Daisy's handwriting she had. They would have the means to have the handwriting on both analyzed, and maybe Daisy could be exonerated.

"I didn't tell you," Joy said after a moment, "but I went to talk to the clerk at the florist shop."

"What did she say? Who bought the flowers?"

"It was a woman, but it was raining that day, and the woman had a raincoat on and a scarf over her hair and was wearing glasses. The clerk said that she couldn't tell a lot about her besides that she was unremarkable."

The corner of Veronica's mouth twitched. "That's too bad. I was hoping she could be identified. She didn't leave a name either?"

"No. The woman paid cash and wrote the card right there."

"She might never be found." Veronica glanced out the windows toward Connor's door and then rubbed her temples. "With everything that's been going on, my nerves are shot. I'm so tired of all this."

"That's understandable. You've had a lot to deal with."

"I wish I could forget about this crazy person who's trying to hurt my son and just be glad he's all right. As long as he's okay, nothing else matters, right?"

"Have you decided you don't want the police to be involved?" Joy asked uneasily.

"No. I want whoever this is to be stopped, whatever it takes. As much as I don't want to deal with it anymore, I have to protect Connor."

"Why don't you go nap for a while in his room?" Joy stood up. "That way he won't be alone, but you can get some rest at the same time."

"All right." Veronica got to her feet too. "That would be nice. Do I need to call the police?"

"I think you should make a report, but if you like, I can talk to Rebekah informally and get some advice on what you ought to do."

"I'd really appreciate that. I'll be in Connor's room if she wants to talk to me right away." Veronica squeezed Joy's hand. "Thank you for all your help."

"You're welcome."

Joy walked with her across the hall and opened the door to let her into the room. Once she had taken a quick peek at Connor, still sleeping soundly, she pulled the door shut and went back into the waiting room to call Rebekah. She had a lot to talk to her about.

Chapter Twelve

JOY SCROLLED THROUGH HER PHONE'S list of contacts and found Detective Rebekah Osborne's.

She picked up the phone almost immediately. "Detective Osborne."

"Rebekah, hi. It's Joy Atkins at Mercy Hospital."

"Oh hey, Joy. How are you?"

"I'm doing fine, but there's been something going on up here, and I was hoping to ask you about it before there's an actual formal report filed."

"Okay," she said cautiously. "Tell me about it."

"Are you busy? It would be better if you could come see some evidence I have."

"I was about to take my break. Sure, I can come up. Do you want me to meet you at the gift shop?"

"Actually, no. If you don't mind, can you meet me in the waiting room next to Room 220 on the second floor? I'll explain everything when you get here."

A few minutes later, Joy saw Rebekah walking down the hallway. She got up and opened the door for her.

"Thanks for coming. I'm sorry this coffee isn't quite as good as what we have at the gift shop, but I'd be happy to pour you some."

"Only if you'll join me," she said with a smile.

"I think I could use a cup."

She poured out two and brought them along with sugar and creamer to the coffee table in front of where Rebekah was sitting.

"Thanks." Rebekah added creamer to her cup and then took a grateful sip. "I haven't had a break since six this morning. This is exactly what I needed."

"No lunch?"

She chuckled. "I grabbed a burger in between crime scenes. So, what have you got for me?"

Joy nodded toward the room across the hall. "There's a boy, almost sixteen, in that room, Room 214. His name is Connor Sherman. Originally, he was here for knee surgery, but Thursday somebody sent an arrangement of daisies up to his room. He's allergic to daisies and had a reaction to them. He was all right, but with that and recovering from surgery and some tests one of his doctors wanted to run, he spent the weekend here instead of going home."

"Okay, and?"

"Earlier today, he ate a piece of candy, the kind of candy he's been eating for years, and he had another allergic reaction. More severe this time."

Rebekah's forehead wrinkled. "How is he?"

"He's recovering. Sleeping now, I think. His mother's with him."

"So what are you saying? That someone wants to harm him?"

"That's what it seems like to me. Whoever this is might want to keep him in the hospital for a while, maybe even convince him that he needs to stay home and not try to get into college. Maybe even not work so hard at school so he won't be valedictorian and get the scholarship that goes with it."

"He must be pretty smart if he's trying to get into college before he's even sixteen," Rebekah said.

"He's very smart. In fact, he has a doctor studying him and a filmmaker doing a documentary on him. Both of them have been studying him since he was very little."

Rebekah narrowed her eyes. "What happens to them if the kid goes off to school?"

"That's exactly what I've been wondering. It would make it much harder for them to complete the projects they've been working on all these years."

"Decent motive. Do you have any evidence against them?"

"Not really. The filmmaker brought the chocolates for him, but she had a reaction to it too. You know Dr. Morton. He took the candy to be analyzed. He found that all the pieces had been injected with a small amount of peanut oil, something both victims are highly allergic to."

"Are you saying someone is after this filmmaker?"

"No," Joy said. "I don't think so anyway. She wasn't even around when the flowers were delivered, and I don't think she has a problem with daisies, but that brings me to another suspect, and this is where the evidence comes in."

"And it is?"

Rebekah sipped her coffee as Joy got the florist's card and the notepad from her purse.

"This was on the flowers," Joy said, laying the card on the table in front of Rebekah. "And this was written by one of our hospital volunteers."

She put the notepad beside the card, and Rebekah leaned closer to study them both.

"And what does this volunteer have to say about it?" Rebekah asked.

"She has no explanation. She was the one who delivered the flowers up to the room, that's something our volunteers do regularly, but she says she absolutely didn't write the card or buy the flowers. So either she did it and is lying about it for some reason, or someone else wanted everyone to think she did it. Either way, it wasn't an innocent mistake."

"Have you checked with the flower shop?"

"I have," Joy said, "but the woman there couldn't tell me much about the purchaser except it was a woman and that she paid cash for the arrangement and had them send it for her to the hospital."

"Do you know where the filmmaker was that morning?"

"No, I haven't asked her that. I don't know if she's actually a suspect. She's been following Connor for years, and they seem to be on good terms. He told her he probably wasn't going to keep being filmed much longer, and she seemed to take it in stride. She's not happy about it, of course, but she seemed to understand."

"The research doctor couldn't have been the one at the flower shop?" Rebekah asked.

"No. He's a big man with a full beard. The clerk at the florist's was sure a woman bought the flowers and wrote the card."

"He could have had someone take care of it for him, you know. Does he have a wife? A daughter?"

Joy winced. "I hadn't thought as far as that. It would certainly make this harder to trace."

Rebekah took a drink of her coffee and was silent for a moment. "What about the kid's folks? What are they like?"

"His father died three or four years ago," Joy said. "His mother is one of my neighbors, though we really hadn't talked much until now. She's one of those helicopter parents, always hovering. My guess is that she's part of the reason her son is so eager to not have all this special attention anymore. I can tell they love each other, and he doesn't want to hurt her feelings, but I think, more than most boys his age, he's eager for a little bit of breathing room."

"Any chance she's behind these little 'accidents'?"

Joy thought about what Veronica had said only a few minutes ago about not finding out who had been behind the incidents as long as Connor was all right. Joy could understand someone in her position not wanting to deal with the problem anymore, but would someone as perpetually worried as Veronica was about her son really not insist on knowing who was behind these potentially fatal attacks on him?

"Why would you say that?" Joy asked Rebekah.

Rebekah shrugged. "I don't know. A widow with a son who's growing up. Does she have any other kids?"

"She has a daughter already in college."

"And nobody else?"

"Not that I know of," Joy said. "But I haven't seen any evidence that tells me she's anything but a concerned mother."

"And the boy doesn't show any sign of being abused? No bruises? Not withdrawn?"

"Not that I can tell." Joy had heard about parents and other caregivers who deliberately made their charges sick. Surely that wasn't the case here. "He seems pretty well adjusted for someone who's been treated like a star his whole life. And I can't imagine, after all the intense scrutiny he's undergone for years, that someone wouldn't have noticed something by now. Dr. Morton is his GP. I'm sure he would have been asking questions if there was even a hint of anything like that. I would call Child Protective Services myself if I thought there was a reason to."

Rebekah nodded toward the card and the notepad still on the table. "So the only sure evidence that something is actually wrong is the flowers and the peanut oil in the candy. Are you sure the candymaker didn't simply change the recipe?"

"I haven't talked to them or anything, but there's no mention of peanuts on the ingredients list, and Dr. Morton says the oil was injected into the candies. That wouldn't be something the candymaker would do."

Rebekah nodded slowly. "Did Dr. Morton say there was a dangerous amount of peanut oil in the chocolates?"

"Actually, he said there was very little. Connor's really sensitive to it, so it didn't take very much to affect him."

"And the daisies?"

"Just having them in the room was evidently enough to cause problems. Connor was asleep when they were delivered, so he wouldn't have touched them or anything."

"It seems like the perpetrator must be very familiar with the boy's medical history. He or she would have to know exactly how much of a particular substance he could be exposed to without causing a fatal reaction."

"That pretty much applies to everyone involved," Joy admitted.

"Even the girl?"

Joy had to think for a moment about that. "It does sound kind of sophisticated for her. But she and Connor are classmates, and she's very intelligent in her own right. And there's that florist's card to be explained away, so I can't say for certain she couldn't be the one. She mentioned that Connor divulged that he's allergic to various things when he was talking to her in class."

Rebekah picked up the card. "If she didn't write this, then how was someone else able to make this look so much like her writing?"

"That's what puzzles me. She does have to sign in when she comes to do her volunteer work, but only two letters in her name are in that card. It's a million to one shot that someone could fake her writing based only on her signature."

"But she'd have to realize that a handwriting analyst would be able to tell whether or not these were both written by the same person."

"Yes," Joy said, "I'm sure she does."

"I do."

Joy and Rebekah both looked up to see Daisy standing in the doorway to the waiting room.

"I'm sorry," Daisy said, shutting the door behind her. "I didn't mean to listen in, but I heard what happened to Connor, so I went to talk to you, Joy, and Lacy told me you were up here." She saw the card and the notebook on the coffee table and swallowed hard. "I didn't know you'd already have the police looking for me."

Joy held out a hand to her. "Come sit down for a minute. And, no, I don't have the police looking for you. This is Detective Osborne with the Charleston police."

Rebekah nodded at Daisy. "Hi. I'm not here to do anything but find out what's been going on. You tell me the truth, and you'll be okay. So far, nothing too awful has happened to Connor. We only want to make sure that there aren't any more problems, understand?"

"Yes," Daisy said softly. "But I promise I didn't do anything to hurt him. I wouldn't."

"What did you hear about what happened today?" Joy asked her.

"Only that he ate some candy that he had a reaction to, and that lady who's making the film about him did too."

"And where were you today? Have you been at the hospital?"

Daisy nodded. "I got here at about one, and then Polly and I spent a little while doing filing in the administrator's office. And then Ms. Kingston came and got me because Mr. Billingsly wanted me to read to him again. I was with him until I heard about what happened to Connor a little while ago, and that's when I came looking for you."

"And you weren't in Connor's room today?" Joy asked.

Daisy shook her head.

"Not at all?"

"I swear. I never went in there today. The last time I was in there was when I delivered those stupid flowers."

"Do you know anything else about what happened to Connor today, Daisy?" Rebekah asked. "Anything more specific? The kind of candy? What he was allergic to?"

Again, Daisy shook her head. "Only he was allergic to some candy he ate. That's all."

"Do you know how to use a syringe?"

Daisy frowned. "My mom's diabetic, and she taught me how to give her her shots in case she couldn't do it."

Rebekah glanced at Joy.

"What?" Daisy asked. "Does that have something to do with Connor? Did somebody inject him with something he's allergic to?"

"No," Joy told her. "And Connor is doing all right now. He's recovering, so you don't have to worry about him."

Daisy exhaled. "Good. I was scared when I heard something else had happened to him."

"So," Rebekah said, "we were just talking about this card." She picked up the florist's card that had what looked like Daisy's writing on it. "What do you think we'd find out if we had an expert compare this to the one you wrote?"

"That it's not my writing."

There was no hesitation in her voice. She didn't look away from Rebekah's steady gaze.

"Do you have any idea who could imitate your writing like this?" Rebekah asked her.

"No. I'm sorry. I don't have an explanation. I just know I didn't write that." She took a deep breath. "I didn't write that. I didn't send those flowers. And I didn't even see Connor today or go into his room."

There were tears standing in her eyes now, but she still didn't look away.

"It's all right, Daisy," Joy said. "We'll figure it out."

"Okay," she murmured.

Rebekah's expression softened. "I understand you and Connor are classmates. Do you talk much?"

"A little. Not outside of school or anything." Daisy blinked and wiped her eyes. "Um, I think he's going to leave school early. Maybe after Christmas. At the end of the school year, for sure. But he doesn't talk to me much anymore."

"Did you know about his allergies?"

Daisy nodded. "I know he's got a lot of them, but I thought he was getting better."

"How often do you remember him being sick before?" Joy asked. "A lot?"

"A couple of years ago, he was sick for about a month. I don't know what it was, and Connor never liked to talk about things like that. That's the worst one I know about. Last winter, he got pneumonia and had to be in the hospital for a few days, and he was out of school for a couple of weeks, but he bounced right back. I don't think he's missed any school since then."

"You said you've only talked with Connor in school," Rebekah said. "You've never been to his house or had him over to yours?"

"No. Nothing like that."

"You haven't, maybe with a group of friends, gone with him to the mall or to a school football game or something?"

"No," Daisy said. "I guess if you count a pep rally, we sat next to each other once about a year ago, but that was all. He didn't even talk to me."

"All right. Is there anything else you'd like to tell me? Anything at all that might help us figure out what's going on here?"

"I don't know anything to say. I'd help you if I could, but I've told you everything."

"Thanks for your cooperation." Rebekah gave Daisy one of her business cards. "If you think of anything at all, you give me a call right away, okay?"

"Okay."

Daisy clutched the card in her hand.

"Let me get your full name and address and phone number too," Rebekah said.

Daisy wrote them all down for her on the same pad she had written on earlier.

"Thanks. You can get back to work now if you like."

Daisy stood up and looked at Joy. "I wouldn't do something like this. Really."

"We'll find out what happened," Joy told her. "It'll be all right. You'd better get back to Mr. Billingsly now. He seems like a really nice man. I'd like to meet him sometime."

Daisy beamed at her. "You ought to come visit. He'd love that. I'll see you later."

Joy watched as Daisy hurried out the doorway, past the corridor windows, and was gone.

"What do you think?" she asked Rebekah.

"You're right. She doesn't seem like the type. In my experience, that doesn't mean much, but she really doesn't seem like the type."

"So what do we do now?"

"If the boy's mother wants to open an investigation, I'll have a talk with Dr. Morton. Then I'll probably see what I can find out from your other suspects, the filmmaker and the research doctor. And I'll check out the mom while I'm at it."

"I suppose that's the only logical thing to do. I can't believe it would be any of them, but then again, I don't know who would have a reason to do anything to Connor unless it's one of them or Daisy."

"I understand that the three adults each have a reason for keeping Connor around longer than he wants to stay, but what about the girl?"

"The only thing I can figure out is that she could be jealous because he's going to be valedictorian instead of her and they're competing for the same very lucrative scholarship. He's about a year younger than she is, so there might be a little bit of embarrassment in play because of that too."

Joy paused for a moment, not knowing whether or not to bring this up, but Rebekah needed all the facts if her inquiry was going to do anybody any good.

"There was a letter that Daisy brought to Connor last Wednesday," she said finally.

"A letter?"

"It was an invitation for him to tour one of the colleges and talk to them about a possible scholarship. Daisy said she noticed it in the trash in here. She recognized the school logo and thought it was important, so she brought it back to him. Connor's mother was very upset and claimed that Daisy had stolen the letter to keep him from getting it. Daisy said if she had done that, it didn't make sense that she would have brought it back."

"And what did the mother say?"

"She claimed that Daisy was afraid she'd get caught and get in trouble, so she pretended she found it in the trash."

"She could be right." Rebekah got up and topped off her coffee and then sat down again. "But so could the girl. Who else would have had a reason to get rid of that letter?"

"Evidently any of them, if they don't want Connor to go away to school anytime soon. I think the mail was left in Connor's room, so again, anyone could have gotten that letter. I realize that's not much to go on."

Rebekah smiled. "Most of the time, it's the little things that add up in an investigation that help us nail the bad guy. If you ask me, the best thing you can do to help is keep your eyes and ears open and let us know if you find any more clues."

"I'll stay in touch."

Once she was gone, Joy decided to go check on Veronica and Connor. She didn't like the idea that a mother would purposely harm her own child. She had seen no evidence of that with Veronica, but the idea bothered her. As Rebekah had advised, she'd keep her eyes and ears open.

Chapter Thirteen

Joy went across the hall from the waiting room to Connor Sherman's door. It remained closed, and as far as she knew, Connor and his mother were both still sleeping. It would probably be best if she came back later. She needed to talk things over with Shirley, Anne, and Evelyn anyway.

She was about to turn around and walk toward the elevator when the door silently opened. Connor stood there supported by his crutches, his hand wrapped around his IV pole and a mug hanging off one finger and a startled look on his face.

"Hey," he said softly. "I didn't know anybody was out here."

"Connor. I didn't mean to disturb you. I was wondering how you were doing, but I didn't want to knock in case you and your mother were asleep."

He jiggled the empty mug. "I was only going to get some ice from the dispenser."

"I'm sure one of the nurses would have gotten it for you."

"Yeah, but I'm going crazy sitting in there doing nothing. I can't even watch TV or anything, because it would wake up Mom. I thought I could at least stretch my legs." He grinned a little. "Leg."

"I don't blame you, but is it a good idea for you to be up with no one knowing?"

"It's all right. I'm being careful."

Joy looked at him dubiously. "How are you feeling?"

"I'm fine." He came out into the hallway, a little wobbly on his crutches.

"Do you need help?" Joy asked him.

"Nah. The ice maker is just a couple of doors down. But I'd better not get caught. I've been warned once."

"What if I get the ice for you and you can go back and lie down before anybody sees you?"

Connor made a face. "Can't I just walk a little bit?"

"What if I go talk to your nurse and see if it's okay if I walk with you? That way if you need help, you won't be alone."

He huffed. "You can walk with me, but don't get the nurse, okay? She'll have a fit."

"And if you fall, I'll get fired."

Joy scurried over to the nurses' station and told the nurse on duty what was going on.

The nurse sighed. "Stay with him, and I'll get a wheelchair. And tell him I'll be in his room in a minute to make sure everything's okay and read him the riot act. He's been trying to get out of here for days now. I don't know if we can keep him down much longer."

"Just so you'll know, his mother is still asleep in his room. We wanted to talk and not disturb her."

"You can push him around in a chair and still talk." The nurse went to get a wheelchair. "I'll be by there in a minute, Joy. Keep him from going anywhere."

Joy nodded and went back to where Connor still waited for her.

"Am I in trouble?" he asked.

"Definitely," Joy said with a smile. "But she said you could be up, as long as you use the wheelchair the nurse is bringing. You're lucky she's so nice."

"Yeah, she is. They all are. But I want to go home."

"They understand that, but you have to understand that they're responsible for you, and they don't want you to hurt yourself."

"I didn't take the IV out like I wanted to," he protested.

Joy shook her head. "You're supposed to be the smart one. At least you realized that wasn't a good idea."

"I didn't do it, all right? That doesn't mean I didn't want to."

"I heard that," the nurse said, coming up with the wheelchair. She settled him in the chair and stashed the crutches back in his room. "Stop messing with things, and you'll get out of here faster. And somebody will be happy to get you ice water anytime you want it, okay?"

"Okay," Connor said with a smile that was apologetic and mischievous at the same time.

The nurse smiled too. "Be good now, and don't give Joy any trouble."

Connor didn't make any promises.

"As long as you're out here," Joy said once the nurse was gone, "let's get your ice water. But we'd better not be gone long. If your mother wakes up and you're not there, she's going to be upset."

"Poor Mom. I wish she didn't worry about me so much."

Joy wheeled him down the hall the IV stand trailing next to them. "That's what moms do."

He shook his head. "Not this much. I mean, I'm practically grown up, and she treats me like I'm two."

Joy didn't want to make him think his mother would do even the slightest thing to harm him, but she wanted to know if there was a pattern of these incidents happening before now.

"Do you ever feel like you're about to get everything going the way you want when something comes along to set you back?" she asked after they had passed the little kitchen area with the ice maker in it. They'd come back to it in a few minutes.

"That has happened once in a while, but not much lately," Connor said. "And before it was stuff I could understand, like I actually got sick or something. It wasn't somebody trying to make me sick."

"Is that what you think is happening now?"

He gave her a look that clearly said he wasn't a child anymore and that he wasn't stupid. "It seems pretty obvious, doesn't it?"

"I was only wondering what you were thinking."

He shrugged. "I guess I'm glad that whoever this is doesn't hate me enough to do anything really bad. Either that or he's not very good at this."

"Do you have any enemies you know of? Maybe somebody at school?"

He glanced back at her. "You wonder if it's Daisy too."

"I didn't say that, and I'm not suggesting that. I only want to know what you think."

"Mom thinks it's her. She hasn't said much about it, but I know that's what she thinks." He pressed his lips together. "I don't think it's Daisy. That wouldn't be like her."

"Did you see the card that was on the flowers that were delivered to you?"

"Mom showed it to me. She wanted to know if I recognized the handwriting." He looked at Joy almost defiantly. "I told her I didn't."

"Is that the truth?"

He let the mild question dangle in the air for a moment, and then he looked away.

"I'm not sure."

Joy waited for him to go on.

"Awhile ago," he began slowly, "I was in the hospital and I got some flowers. These were white carnations with some greenery around them, and there was a card with them."

"What kind of card?"

"Just the little kind that usually comes with flowers. And it had *Get well soon* written on it."

"Who sent it? Do you know?"

He shrugged uneasily. "Not for sure. I kind of thought so though. Nobody ever said anything, but I kept the card. I figured somebody was nice enough to care about what happened to me."

"What happened to the card?" Joy asked. "Do you still have it at home?"

"That's the thing. I've been using it for a bookmark for a long time. I had it in the book I've been reading here at the hospital, but then I lost it."

"You mentioned one of the nurses getting you a new one. Did anybody see what happened to the old one? Do you know?"

"No. It's gone. Maybe it fell out and got swept up or something."

"And you never found out who sent it?"

He shook his head. "Here's the thing, and I don't want you to tell Mom, okay?"

"I can't promise you that," she said seriously. "Not if it helps with figuring out what's been going on."

"Okay."

They went down to the end of the hallway and turned around without saying anything else. She couldn't force him to talk if he didn't want to, but she wondered if he had recognized or if he thought he'd recognized the handwriting on the recent florist's card. She wondered too what that had to do with the earlier card.

"You don't have to answer if you don't want to," she said as they approached the kitchen area again, "but you said that the first card had *Get well soon* written on it. I'm wondering now if you recognized that handwriting. Maybe when you got the first one, and maybe when you saw the second one recently. It had *Get well soon* written on it too."

Joy turned him into the kitchen area. It was only a little room off the hallway with a small counter and upper and lower cabinets, a refrigerator, a microwave, and a coffee maker. He filled his mug with ice and then water from the refrigerator door and then she turned him to go back out to the hallway.

"I talked to Daisy about you," Joy said.

"You did?"

"She said she thought you were friends, but then you wouldn't talk to her anymore. Did she do something to make you mad?"

He shook his head, his fingers tightening on the IV stand. "Look," he said, exhaling heavily, "she was nice to me in class. That's all. That doesn't mean she—" He bit his lip. "It doesn't mean she's out to get me or something. I don't know why anybody would think that."

"I'm only trying to find out what happened," Joy said gently. "I'm not trying to be nosy, okay?"

He gave her a grudging smile. "Sure. I don't know what to tell you, except I don't think Daisy would do something like that. That's all. And I don't know who would. It doesn't make sense to me."

"All right. We'll leave it at that. Friends?"

"Yeah, friends."

They went down to his room, and she stopped him in front of the still-closed door.

"Listen," he said. "I appreciate that you're trying to help. And I know Mom's glad to have somebody to talk to. And she's glad you're trying to find out what's going on. It's kind of scary when you get a reaction like that sometimes. You think you're never going to get a deep breath ever again. So yeah, I'm grateful too, and I don't want something like this to happen anymore. But I don't want anybody to get blamed for something somebody else did, okay?"

"I don't want that either," Joy said. "Nobody does."

"Anyway, I'd better get back into bed before the nurse comes in and doesn't have anybody to yell at."

Joy chuckled. "Maybe you'd better. But please be careful from now on. We don't want anything to happen to you."

"Yeah, I know. Mom would—"

He broke off when the door flew open. Veronica stood there, her hair disheveled and her eyes wide.

"Oh," she said on a breath. "I thought something else happened to you. Why didn't you let me know you got up?"

"Mom," Connor said with an uncomfortable glance at Joy, "I only went down the hall to get some ice water. Joy and I were talking, and we didn't want to wake you up, and I wanted to get a little change of scenery. I've been cooped up in there for a long time."

Veronica smiled sheepishly and started to pat her hair into place. "I think I'm still half asleep anyway. I didn't mean to overreact. Won't you come in, Joy?"

"Why don't you go back and lie down now, Connor?" Joy suggested. "I'd like to talk to your mother again."

"About me?" Connor asked warily.

"About what's been happening to you, yes."

"Is it something I can't know about?"

"That would be up to your mother, I think."

Connor looked at Veronica expectantly.

Veronica turned and went back into the room, and Joy rolled Connor in after her. With a sigh, she sank down into the chair she had no doubt been sleeping in.

"I guess I'm going to have to face the fact that you're growing up now, Connor. Faster than I ever thought you would. I suppose you have a right to know what's going on as much as anybody else."

"I think so," he said quietly.

"Get back into bed, and we'll both find out what Joy has to say."

Connor pressed the button on the remote control until the head of the bed was almost straight up. Then he got under the sheet.

Joy sat down in the chair opposite Veronica's. "I don't have much information to give you yet. I did talk to my police officer friend, Rebekah Osborne. She'll probably want to come talk to both of you."

"Good," Veronica said.

"There's something else I told her about," Joy said. "I talked to Daisy about that card that came with the flowers. I had her write

Get well soon on a piece of paper for me. It looked very much like what was written on that card."

Veronica's eyes flashed. "I knew it was her."

"It's a mistake," Connor said at once.

"Why do you say that?"

"It just is. Daisy wouldn't do that. I told you already."

"Then how do you explain the handwriting being so much like hers?"

"I don't know. Why do you have to pick on Daisy? You don't even know her."

"I'm sorry."

Joy didn't dare say anything right then.

"I wish I knew what happened to that little card you were using for a bookmark," Veronica said, her tone suddenly bright. "That one said the same thing. It would be interesting to know if the handwriting matches the one you got last week."

Connor ducked his head and didn't say anything. What was it about that particular card that Connor didn't want anyone to know?

"You should have seen him looking for that card the other day," Veronica said. "You'd have thought it was autographed by some movie star or something."

"It was only a card," he said, almost sullenly. "I don't know why you have to make a big deal about it."

"Now, I'm not trying to make a big deal about it, honey. It was getting pretty battered anyway. I don't know why you held on to it this long. Did you ever figure out who that was from?"

"No."

"But your nurse was very nice to get you a new bookmark."

"Yeah."

Nobody said anything for a moment.

"Maybe you should rest for a while," Veronica suggested. "We can talk to Joy later."

"I haven't done anything but rest all this time," Connor snapped. Then he took a deep breath. "I'm sorry, Mom, but I'd really like to hear what happened with the police. And I'm not tired, okay?"

Veronica nodded.

"The police will probably have the handwriting on the card and the notepad analyzed," Joy told them. "So that will determine whether or not Daisy wrote the card."

"Good," Connor said. "Because I don't think it was her."

Veronica frowned but said nothing.

"Daisy talked to Rebekah too," Joy said. "She says she doesn't know anything about the card or why it looks like her writing." She considered for a moment. "Connor, do you remember when you last had the card you were using for a bookmark?"

"I don't know. I had it when I came to the hospital, because I was almost through with the book I was reading. I didn't pick up the book again until that night, but the card was gone."

"So it was taken from your room here at the hospital."

"Yeah. It had to have been."

"Do you remember where you left your book the last time you had the card?"

He put his hand on the table next to the bed. "Right here."

"And was the book there the next time you wanted it?"

"Yeah. I don't remember thinking it had been moved or anything. But when I opened it to read, the card was gone."

"Who had been in your room before then?" Joy asked him. "Do you remember?"

Connor wrinkled his forehead for a moment. "Dr. Morton came in for a while. The nurses. Dr. Dahlman was here, telling me what all he was planning to do as far as testing was concerned. Swarna filmed him and me while that was going on. I think that's all. Do you remember anybody else, Mom?"

"Not off the top of my head," Veronica said.

"Were either or both of you in the room the whole time?" Joy asked. "I mean between the time you put your bookmark in place and put the book down, and the next time you picked the book up and saw the card wasn't there."

Veronica and Connor looked at each other questioningly.

"I think we were," she said finally. "I remember getting Connor's things put up the way he likes them. All the toiletries in the bathroom and that kind of thing."

"Mom," he protested. "Nobody cares about that."

"Well, I was only trying to remember. After Swarna filmed Dr. Dahlman, they both left. Dr. Morton came and went after that."

"Before that," Connor reminded her.

"Was it?"

"Yes, because the technician he sent to get me for the electrocardiogram had to wait a few minutes until Swarna was finished filming."

Veronica nodded. "Yes, I remember now. So I guess, Joy, we actually were gone for a little while that day. Not long though."

"Long enough," Joy said. "The question now is why someone would want to take that card out of Connor's book." She looked at Connor. "Are you sure there's nothing you can tell us about the card?"

Connor looked at her warily, but she kept her expression merely pleasant. She knew there was something that he didn't want his mother to know, but she wouldn't repeat what he had said to her earlier about it or even indicate that he had basically admitted there was something he had wanted to say. Still, she hoped he would reconsider and tell her and Veronica both what it was.

Connor raked his fingers through his thick hair. "It was just a card. It wasn't signed. It wasn't anything, and it was a long time ago."

"How long ago?"

"I don't know. Maybe this time last year."

Clearly, he wasn't going to say anything else about it.

"Let's talk about the candy then," Joy said. "You said Swarna has given you that kind before. Always the same brand? Or has it been different?"

"I think it's always the same kind," Connor told her. "I would have noticed if it was a different brand."

"He always notices," Veronica put in. "One time they changed the style of the print on the box, and he asked Swarna if it was a different kind of candy."

"Do you know anything about where it's made?" Joy asked.

Connor shook his head. "I know it's one of those fancy places that makes the chocolates by hand. At least that's what Swarna says. It's her favorite place."

"It's a shame, really," Veronica said, "because one of the reasons she buys from them is that they use all fresh, organic ingredients and no preservatives. She's like Connor, very sensitive."

Connor's look of annoyance was only fleeting.

"Have you heard from her since she was in the ER?" Joy asked. "Is she doing all right?"

"Actually, she's supposed to come up and film that interview with Dr. Morton today," Veronica said. "She seems eager to get to work. She said she's doing fine now."

"Are you going to get to go home today, Connor?" Joy asked. "Finally?"

He exhaled, making the lock of hair that had fallen over his forehead bounce upward. "I hope so. Mom's going to ask after Swarna talks to Dr. Morton. I'm really ready to not be here anymore."

Joy patted his shoulder. "I have to go talk to Dr. Morton anyway. I'll tell him you sure don't look like somebody who ought to be taking up a valuable hospital bed."

He grinned. "That'd be great."

Joy went straight from Connor's room to Dr. Morton's office. His nurse was away from her desk, so Joy walked up to his inner-office door to knock. She stopped when she heard a voice from the other side of the door.

"I want you to keep him here at least until tomorrow, the later the better."

That wasn't Dr. Morton. She was almost positive it was Dr. Dahlman.

Chapter Fourteen

"He's pretty eager to get out of here."

Joy could hear Dr. Morton's voice through his office door, though it wasn't as strident as Dr. Dahlman's. She was sure they were talking about Connor.

"I realize that," Dr. Dahlman said. "But I wanted to do a sleep study tonight. I get the feeling he's not going to put up with me much longer."

"That's possible, I suppose," Dr. Morton said. "But that doesn't have anything to do with what would be best for him medically at this point. And shouldn't your tests and anything else of this nature be up to him?"

"Well, of course. But I'm not asking for weeks or months. Just another night. Are you sure he's totally recovered from that last allergic reaction? Shouldn't he have multiple IV fluid boluses to treat his hypotension resulting from the reaction?"

"I've been going over his chart, trying to decide if that's necessary at this point. His blood pressure has improved almost to normal." Dr. Morton paused for a moment. "I could release him with Medrol and Benadryl."

Joy recognized the medications. Medrol was a steroid, and Benadryl was an antihistamine.

"And," Dr. Morton added, "I would give his mother strict instructions to keep an EpiPen nearby and bring him back to the ER if the symptoms recur. He has had a history of that, though the last few times he's needed treatment, he didn't have a recurrence. That's why I was thinking of releasing him."

"But it wouldn't be unwarranted to keep him under observation for a full twenty-four hours from the incident, would it?"

"No. I can't say I haven't considered that, just in an abundance of caution."

"And that would suit both of us, and then Connor wouldn't have to spend the night in a clinic having this sleep study done. He'd already be settled in here."

Dr. Morton chuckled. "If you put it that way, I suppose I'd be doing him a favor by keeping him. That is, *if* he was going to agree to your sleep study anyway."

Before Dr. Dahlman could respond, Joy heard someone start to open the outer office door, and she stepped quickly to the other side of the room before Dr. Morton's nurse came in.

"Joy. I didn't expect to see you here. How are you?"

"Hi, Milly," Joy said. "I just stopped by to see the doctor, but I think there's someone in his office with him. I was hoping you'd be back so I could see when Dr. Morton will be available."

"Oh, that's just Dr. Dahlman," Milly told her as she sat in the chair behind her desk. "He's in and out of here all the time if Connor Sherman is in the hospital. He usually doesn't stay long. If you'd like to wait, Dr. Morton should be out in a few minutes. Or I can leave him a message to call you, if you'd prefer."

"I'll wait a few minutes," Joy said, sitting down too. "Do you know if Rebekah Osborne came by here earlier today?"

"The detective? Yes, she was here. She and Dr. Morton talked for some time. Dr. Morton gave her the results for the analysis of the candies Connor and Swarna LeFrye ate and the reactions they both had to them. He wasn't the doctor who treated Ms. LeFrye, but he did consult with him, a Dr. Powell. She didn't have as bad a time as Connor did."

Right then, Dr. Morton's door opened and he and Dr. Dahlman came out.

"Hello, Joy," Dr. Morton said. "I didn't expect to see you up here. Is everything all right?"

"I was hoping I could talk to you for only a minute if you have time."

Dr. Morton glanced at his watch. "I've got to do an interview. Can you make it quick?"

She had wanted to ask a few more questions about his analysis of the candy, but maybe this wasn't the best time. She didn't want to say the wrong thing in front of Dr. Dahlman either in case he actually had something to do with what had been going on.

"I can always come back another time," she said. "I was just talking to Connor, and I promised him I would tell you he's too healthy to still be in the hospital."

Dr. Morton laughed softly. "To tell the truth, he is, but I was talking to Dr. Dahlman, and he's convinced me it would be better if he lets us observe him for another night. Just to be careful."

"But Swarna went home already."

"True, but she didn't have as severe a reaction, and she is generally much stronger than Connor is."

"I suppose you're right."

"And actually," Dr. Dahlman said, "since Dr. Morton let me know he was going to keep Connor overnight, I've decided to do another study I've been wanting to do for a while. I figure he'll be happier about staying if he realizes that if he does the study tonight, he won't have to do it some other time. He'll be killing two birds with one stone, as it were."

Joy didn't think it had originally been Dr. Morton's decision to keep Connor overnight, and she didn't think Dr. Dahlman had decided to do the study based on that decision, but she didn't say anything. She did wonder why Dr. Dahlman hadn't quite told the truth about it. Maybe he didn't want to make it look like he had gotten Dr. Morton to change his mind on the issue. Maybe he had another reason.

"Connor's not going to be happy about it," she said, "but I think you're right that he'll be glad he can do your study now, when he has to stay anyway."

The outer office door opened, and Swarna came in. Her abundant hair was twisted into a low bun at the base of her neck, a much more polished look than Joy had seen before. Her outfit was colorful, boldly graphic, and her makeup, though subtle, looked as if it had been professionally applied. Evidently her medical emergency earlier in the day seemed to have done her very little harm.

"I hope I'm not late," she said breathlessly, and she moved the large messenger bag she was carrying up to her shoulder.

"A little early, in fact," Dr. Morton said.

"Hello, Dr. Dahlman. Joy." Swarna nodded at each of them in turn. "I didn't expect to find a party going on."

"Nothing as glamorous as that," Dr. Dahlman said. "How are you feeling?"

"Oh, you know. Not at my best, but the show must go on. I have a friend who's a wonderful makeup artist. She's good enough to help me out when I'm going to be on camera."

"We can put this off until you're feeling better," Dr. Morton said.

"Oh no." Swarna shook one slender finger at him. "It's been hard enough to get you to agree to this. I might never catch you again."

"I didn't realize you were going to be in this film too," Joy said. "Don't you have a crew?"

"No, but I'm not in much of the film," Swarna told her. "If I'm going to do an interview, I like to be face-to-face with my subject if I can, but I'm in charge of recording for all my films. I'll be setting up a camera and then simply letting it go while Dr. Morton and I talk."

Dr. Morton straightened his tie. "Maybe I should have spruced myself up a little before now."

"You're fine." Swarna shifted the bag over her shoulder and then took his arm. "You look great, and this won't take very long at all."

"I hope you both enjoy the interview," Dr. Dahlman said. "I'm going to go give Connor the bad news."

"Bad news?"

"Dr. Morton is keeping him overnight for observation."

Swarna shook her head. "He's not going to like that."

"I'll be doing a sleep study while he's here too. Might as well get some good out of it if he has to be here anyway."

"You'll be doing the study in his room?" Swarna asked.

"I have some equipment I can bring in without too much trouble. That way there will be no need to interfere with what Dr. Morton is doing."

"Mostly I want to keep him on fluids and monitor what's going on," Dr. Morton said. "There's not much to that. I'll send him home tomorrow. To be honest, I don't expect to see him again for some time, barring another unforeseen incident."

"I'm sure his mother will be with him the entire time," Dr. Dahlman said. "Even when I'm not there. So he ought to be all right."

Swarna considered for a moment. "When were you planning to start your test? I think I'd like to include some of that in my film. You know, what you're doing, what you're looking for, all that. Do you think I could film you setting up and then come in the morning to talk to you and Connor about what it was like and how you think it went?"

"You'll have to clear that with him and Veronica, of course, but I have no objection."

"What *are* you looking for, Dr. Dahlman?" Joy asked.

"I've compiled an extended audio file with a variety of input," he said. "Some of it is music, some of it is literature, some of it is mathematical or logistical problems or theoretical discussion. Each of them ranges from quite simple to extremely complex. I want to see how Connor's brain responds to them during sleep."

"I definitely need to include that in my film," Swarna said, her eyes alight.

"I'll mention it to Veronica and Connor. I doubt that will be a problem."

"Maybe I'll come by and check with them after I've finished my interview with Dr. Morton, just to make sure I'm prepared if they're okay with me coming back when you start tonight."

He gave her a wry smile. "You'd better get in all the filming you can while you can. I think our boy is trying to kick over the traces these days."

"Tell me about it."

Dr. Morton cleared his throat. "If we could, I'd like to get started on the interview. I have a meeting coming up later on."

"Let's get going then," Swarna said. "I don't want to make you late. Dr. Dahlman, I'll see you soon. Bye, Joy."

"Bye," Joy said. "Enjoy your interview, Dr. Morton."

Dr. Morton grumbled and escorted Swarna into his office.

"Mind if I walk with you back to Connor's room?" Joy asked Dr. Dahlman. "I know he and his mother want to know whether he'll be going home tonight."

"Sure. Come on."

They said goodbye to Dr. Morton's nurse and then walked down the hall.

"Maybe you can get Connor to see that staying one more night isn't such a bad thing after all," Dr. Dahlman said. "And I'm sure his mother wouldn't want to risk taking him home if Dr. Morton thinks there might be a problem."

"Still, Connor will be disappointed. He's eager to get out of here and get back to his regular routine." Joy glanced at him as they reached the elevators. "Did he tell you about the letter he got from MIT?"

Dr. Dahlman raised his eyebrows. "No. I'm sure he's excited."

The elevator arrived, and they both stepped inside.

"I think he's very excited to know that someone had basically recommended him."

"What does his mother say about that?"

"I think she gets nervous thinking of him going away to school."

"Which he will, of course, in time. I hope, though, that she won't worry about that right now. The more nervous she gets, the more she clings, and the more Connor resists."

"And that makes it harder for you to do your studies."

The elevator stopped, and they got out and walked to Connor's room. Dr. Dahlman knocked rapidly on the doorframe and then went inside.

"Connor," he said as he approached the bed. "How are you feeling today?"

"All right," Connor said. "Did you talk to Dr. Morton, Joy?"

Joy stood next to Dr. Dahlman. "Yes, I did. He wants you to stay here tonight."

Connor slumped against his pillows. "Man."

"Now, honey," Veronica said. "You don't want anything to happen because you went home too soon, do you?"

"Actually," Dr. Dahlman told her, "this really works out great for both of you."

Connor looked at him warily.

"Seriously," the doctor said. "I talked to Dr. Morton. He said he wants to keep you under observation for twenty-four hours. You know I've been wanting to do that sleep study, right?"

"Yeah."

"Well, we could do that tonight, couldn't we? Then, when you go home, you won't have to come back here or to some clinic to do the study. It's like hitting two birds with one stone. What do you think?"

Connor sighed. "I guess it's better than having to spend two nights in the hospital instead of one."

"There you go. What do you think, Veronica?"

"I was hoping we could spend tonight at home. After what's happened here, I'm not sure I want him staying any longer than necessary."

"You usually stay with him. Could you stay tonight? If so, he wouldn't be alone. And you could arrange for one of the nurses to come in if you needed to be out of the room for a few minutes, couldn't you?"

"Well, I suppose so."

"All right. Then we're all set. I'll be back around ten to set things up. You ought to be nice and sleepy by then."

Connor frowned. "I haven't gone to bed by ten since I *was* ten."

Dr. Dahlman gave him a hearty pat on the shoulder. "Yes, I know you're a night owl. But for tonight, I'd like to see if we can get you to sleep early, all right? So no computer or TV after nine, okay, Mom?"

"All right," Veronica said.

"Nothing that's going to keep him up. Some hot decaf tea or warm milk if he wants it."

Connor made a face.

"I'll make sure he's ready," Veronica promised.

"All right. I'll see you both at ten. Joy, it was good to talk to you again."

"I'm sorry," Joy said once he was gone. "I know you wanted to go home today."

"It's all right," Connor said resignedly. "And he's right, you know. If it wasn't tonight, I'd have to spend another night somewhere besides home, and I'm already here, so…" He shrugged.

"I hope it'll be the last for a long time," Veronica said.

She reached out her hand as if she wanted to smooth back the lock of dark hair that seemed to always fall over his forehead, but then she quickly drew it back.

"I tell you what," she said brightly. "Once you're feeling totally well—"

"I already feel totally well."

"Once Dr. Morton says you're up to it then, we'll sign you up for that driver's ed course you were talking about. How would that be?"

His eyes lit. "That would be great."

"There's a good company I was reading about online, and they'll give you the hours you need to get your driver's license and all the individual attention you need."

"Mom," he protested, "I want to take the course they have at school like everybody else does."

"You don't want that," she told him. "You'd have to get up very early in the morning, and you'd have other kids taking up the instructor's time. I don't think you'd like it."

"You mean you don't think *you'd* like it."

"Now, Connor—"

"You know they won't let you ride with me every time, and that's why you want me to take lessons from somewhere else."

"I wouldn't say anything. I'd just enjoy the ride."

"Mom, no."

He looked at Joy, obviously hoping she'd take his side. She actually did take his side, but she knew it wasn't her place to intervene.

"I'd better let you two hash this out in private," she said. "I really only came down because I told you I'd talk to Dr. Morton about discharging you while I was there."

"He didn't say anything else about the chocolates, did he?" Veronica asked.

"I asked to talk to him, but he was about to do his interview with Swarna, so I told him I'd come back later. Have the police come to interview you both yet?"

Connor perked up a little bit then. "We talked to a detective named Rebekah Osborne. She was pretty cool, but there wasn't very much I could tell her. I didn't see anything unusual. I just ate a piece of candy."

"I still wish I'd been there at the time," Veronica said.

"I'm glad you and Swarna are both all right now," Joy told Connor.

"Oh, I haven't checked on her." Veronica looked even more troubled than she had been already. "How does she look?"

"Actually," Joy said, "pretty stunning. She's all fixed up to be on camera for her interview with Dr. Morton."

"Oh, that makes it extra special. I've seen all of her films, and she almost never appears on camera herself. She told me she doesn't like to turn the equipment over to anyone else."

"I understand that she's planning to set up the camera and then let it run while she and Dr. Morton talk."

"Detective Osborne said she was going to talk to Swarna about the candy too," Connor said. "Did Swarna say anything about that when she was in Dr. Morton's office?"

"She didn't mention it," Joy told him. "Rebekah might not have caught up with her yet."

"Swarna probably can't tell the police anything anyway."

"Maybe not, but I'm sure Rebekah will do all she can to figure out what happened and why. I'm still planning to see what I can find out too."

"I want to know about Daisy Graham," Veronica said tautly. "Where was she when those candies were left unattended?"

Connor bit his lip and didn't say anything.

"She was reading to one of our patients who recently had surgery," Joy told her. She didn't say anything about Daisy already having talked to Rebekah Osborne. "She couldn't have come in here and done something to the candy during the time you and Connor were out of the room."

"Are you sure she was with this patient the whole time?" Veronica asked. "She couldn't have left even for a minute or two?"

"That's possible, I suppose, but she'd have to have known about the candy in the first place, and she would have needed an available syringe of peanut oil. It doesn't seem too likely."

Veronica frowned. "Maybe not."

It did seem pretty far-fetched, but could Daisy have managed it? Maybe Daisy could have carried the peanut oil with her for a while, hoping to inject it into something of Connor's. Maybe she had seen Swarna bringing the box of chocolates to Connor's room. Maybe she had slipped out of Mr. Billingsly's room for only a minute or two.

"Anyway," Joy said, "I have some things I need to take care of right now. I hope your test goes well, Connor. And, Veronica, I hope you and I can have coffee or something soon."

"Oh, I'd like that very much," Veronica said. "I can't thank you enough for trying to help us. I know we've taken up a lot of your time, but I appreciate it more than I can say."

"You're more than welcome. Neighbors ought to be there for neighbors, don't you think?"

Veronica nodded. "I feel bad that I haven't made more of an effort to get to know mine, but with everything Connor has been dealing with, well, you understand."

"I do, but thank God that he seems to be getting better and better all the time."

"Oh, I do. Every day."

"All right, well, I'll see you both soon. If I find out anything new, I'll make sure to let you know. See you both later."

"Bye," Veronica and Connor said almost simultaneously.

Joy went from Connor's room straight to the nurses' station. If anyone would know whether Daisy had left the room when those candies were unattended, it would be the man she was reading to.

Chapter Fifteen

"Hi. Can you tell me what room Mr. Billingsly is in?" Joy asked the nurse at the desk.

The nurse checked her computer. "He's in 297."

"Great. Thanks a lot."

Room 297 was in a different corridor on the same floor and not all that far from Connor's. Joy heard the low sound of a football game broadcast going on before she reached the open door, and she peeped in to see an elderly man lying in the bed with the sheets pulled up to his chest. He was ruddy faced and had a ring of snow-white hair circling his mostly bald head. His eyes were closed.

She started to knock on the doorframe, but she saw that his breathing was slow and even and decided he was probably sleeping. She could come back another time.

"I'm not asleep," he said before she could take more than one step away, though he didn't open his eyes. "You can come in."

"I don't want to bother you," she said softly.

"Nonsense," he said, smiling now. "I always have time for a pretty lady. What can I do for you?"

"My name is Joy Atkins. I work in the gift shop here at the hospital."

"Oh, right. Come sit down. Daisy, my little volunteer, has mentioned you before."

Joy sat. "She's mentioned you to me too. I think she's enjoyed reading to you."

"She's very patient to sit and read to an old man for hours at a time."

"I hope you're enjoying *Curtain*. It's one of my favorites."

"Oh, one of mine too. Hang on." Frowning, he patted his hand over the bed until he found the remote control and then he switched off the television. "Sorry about that. It's an old game, but it's a classic, so I can see what's going on just from hearing it."

"I don't want to interrupt."

"No, no, it's fine. I have a video of it. I can listen to it whenever I like. I was only listening now because it happened to be on the sports station. Anyway, yes, *Curtain* is a favorite of mine. I'm enjoying it even more this time since Daisy is reading it to me. I love hearing what she thinks of it since she's experiencing it for the first time. She's got a sharp mind, that one."

"Yes, she does. Was she visiting you today between twelve and two?"

"As a matter of fact, she was. I didn't tell her, because I didn't want to hurt her feelings, but I'm afraid I fell asleep in the middle of it, right where Colonel Luttrell shoots his wife. I woke up a couple of chapters later, but that was all right. I know the story well enough to slip right back into it without missing a beat."

Joy didn't let her surprise show in her voice. "Did she go back and read what you missed?"

"I don't think she realized I was asleep. She usually doesn't. I don't see much of anything anymore, so I leave my eyes closed a lot."

"Is anybody else usually in your room with you, Mr. Billingsly? Relatives, maybe? Friends?"

"Not really. The nurses. The doctor sometimes. Daisy is the only one who comes to visit. I'm going to miss her once they let me out of here. It's not quite the same when it's only the TV or the radio."

"Do you live alone?" Joy asked him.

"I did till I fell. Now I'm in a care facility. That's what they call it these days. To me, it's an old folks' home. At least I have a couple of buddies there. We play a lot of dominoes. I can feel my way through that game."

No wonder he was so eager to have Daisy's company.

"That sounds fun," Joy said cheerfully. "I'm glad you're getting along well here. You know, Daisy told me how much she likes reading to you and trying to figure out whodunit. She's pretty impressed with your deductive powers."

Mr. Billingsly grinned. "I've been around long enough to know most of the tricks. And if I don't, I've probably already read the book anyway."

"Well, I'll let you get back to your game now."

"Was there something you wanted?" he asked.

She had wanted to ask him about whether Daisy had left the room, but he had already told her that on his own.

"Daisy's said so many nice things about you, I thought I'd come up and meet you myself. I hope you don't mind my dropping by."

"Anytime, Joy. Anytime."

"I'll come back and check on you in the next day or two, if you haven't already left the hospital. Would that be all right with you?"

"I'd enjoy it," he said. "Maybe you can drop by when Daisy's here, and we can all talk."

"It's a date. I'll ask her to let me know next time she plans to read to you, and if I can, I'll come too."

"That would be great." His smile was a little wobbly now. "Thanks."

"No, thank you. I've really enjoyed talking to you. I'll see you soon."

She paused for a moment when she was in the hallway again, waiting until the sound of the football game returned. Then she walked down to the nurse's station.

"Hi," she said. "Do you happen to be Mr. Billingsly's nurse?"

"No, that would be Paige right now. Do you want me to get her for you?"

"No, thanks. She's probably busy. I do have a question that you might be able to answer though."

"All right."

"By the way, I'm Joy Atkins. I work in the gift shop."

"Oh, sure. I've heard about you. I'm Trish Benner. I've been here only a couple of weeks. Paige has been showing me the ropes."

"Good to meet you, Trish. Were you on duty today between twelve and two?"

"Yeah, it's my usual shift."

"I suppose you know Daisy Graham."

"Daisy's the volunteer who reads to Mr. Billingsly, right?"

"That's right. Do you remember seeing her early this afternoon?"

"Yeah, sure. He's always a lot more chipper when she's with him."

"Did you happen to notice when she was there? I mean, when she came and when she left?"

Trish thought for a moment. "Well, I know when she came, because she and I were on the elevator together when I was coming back from lunch, so that was about a quarter till twelve. And I remember checking the time when she left, because Paige usually gets in about two thirty and she still wasn't here. She had a flat and called in a few minutes later."

Between eleven forty-five and two thirty. That meant that Daisy should have been reading to Mr. Billingsly while that box of candy was left unattended in Connor's room.

"Do you know if Daisy was in Mr. Billingsly's room that whole time?" Joy asked. "Did you see her leave, even for a few minutes?"

"I can't tell you that for sure," Trish said. "I wasn't at the desk every minute. I have my own patients to take care of."

"Oh, sure," Joy said, "but did you see Daisy leave Mr. Billingsly's room during that time?"

"No. I don't remember anything but her being on the elevator with me and then her leaving."

"Okay, do you know who else was on duty here then?"

"Gina was. Do you know her?"

"I've seen her around the hospital, but I don't really know her," Joy said. "I suppose she's gone for the day."

"Actually, no. She's doing a double shift so she can have a long weekend. Do you want me to call her?"

"That's all right. I don't want to bother her if she's with a patient. I'll just wait for a minute or two."

"All right."

It was less than a minute later when Gina came up to the desk.

"Gina," Joy said. "Hi."

Gina nodded. "Hi. Aren't you Joy from the gift shop?"

"That's right," Joy said. "Do you have a minute?"

"Sure. What is it?"

"Daisy Graham is one of our hospital volunteers, and she's a friend of mine."

"Yes, I know Daisy. She's been a world of good for Mr. Billingsly."

"I can tell," Joy said. "I was just talking to him about her."

"He's the nicest man. I wish all my patients were like him."

Trish sighed. "Wouldn't that be great?"

"You were here when Daisy was reading to him, weren't you, Gina?" Joy asked. "Early this afternoon? Say between noon and two."

"Yes. Is something wrong?"

"I was wondering if you noticed whether Daisy was in Mr. Billingsly's room the whole time she was here or if she left, maybe only for a few minutes, at some point."

"She might have. We were busy then, but I'm pretty sure I saw her in the hall."

"Do you remember when exactly?"

"Exactly? No. But I want to say it was about one. Mrs. Gutterman was getting antsy because her doctor was supposed to come talk to her 'about twelve thirty,' and it was already nearly one. It took me a few minutes to get her settled down, and then I went to call her doctor for her. That's when I saw Daisy in the hall. I didn't see her go back into Mr. Billingsly's room. Maybe you should ask him about it. He's pretty sharp for not being able to see much."

"He told me he fell asleep when Daisy was reading to him," Joy said. "So I didn't actually ask him."

Gina glanced at Trish and then looked at Joy. "Is Daisy in trouble or something? She's really sweet. We all love her."

Trish nodded.

"She's my friend too," Joy told them, "and I'm just trying to get something straightened out. Has she mentioned to either of you when she thinks she'll be working again?"

"She'll be here tomorrow morning," Gina said. "She got permission to come up here once the doctor examines Mr. Billingsly. If he's okay to be released after that, then they'll send him back to assisted living. He wants to have a chance to tell her goodbye before he goes."

"That's very sweet. I hope it all works out the way they hope it will. And as far as my questions are concerned, all of this could be only a misunderstanding, so please don't mention this conversation to anybody. We don't want Daisy to feel like she's being accused of anything."

"Sure," Trish said.

"Great. I'll make sure to talk to Daisy in the morning too. Thanks for your help."

"Good to meet you, Joy," Trish said.

"You too, Trish. See you both later."

Joy walked to the elevator hoping she had done the right thing. Had it merely slipped Daisy's mind that she'd left Mr. Billingsly's room? Or was there a reason she didn't want anyone to know?

Chapter Sixteen

Joy slumped against the elevator wall as she rode down to the lobby. It was well past her usual time to go home. It was good to have someone like Lacy there to back her up when something unusual came up.

The evening was warm, and she was glad to go into her deliciously cool house and change into something comfortable. She had just gotten herself a cold drink and sat down on the couch when the phone rang. She was happy to see it was Roger.

"Hi," she said. "How's your Monday?"

"Going all right. I just talked to Andre."

Joy winced. The last thing she needed was for the plans for the cake to fall through. "Is something wrong?"

"No. Actually, he called to tell me that he had finished the cake and that it's amazing."

Joy chuckled. "He's not shy, is he?"

"Not about his creations. But as far as I can tell, he always says what he really thinks."

"I'm excited to see it."

"Tomorrow," Roger said. "I think it's going to be a great party. I thought you might be worried about it, so I wanted to let you know we're good to go cake-wise."

"I appreciate it very much. Things have been a little crazy at the hospital, and I'm glad I don't have to worry about the party anymore."

"Is this about your neighbor boy again?"

"I've been so busy trying to figure out what's going on with him, I haven't really had time to keep up with much of anything else."

"What's been going on?" he asked.

She told him about Connor Sherman and his mother. And his doctor. And his film journalist. And his classmate who was possibly also a rival.

"I think I'm worn out even hearing about all that," he said. "Who's your front-runner?"

"I'm not sure yet. I really can't believe it's Daisy. Swarna and Dr. Dahlman both would like to keep Connor around longer than he'd like to be, but they've both been around Connor for years now. It's hard to imagine either of them deliberately hurting him."

"Have you had the handwriting on the card analyzed?"

"I think the police are handling that."

"And what do they say? Are they leaning one way or another?"

"I haven't talked to the detective on the case yet. I'd hate to think it's any of them, honestly. Except for Daisy, they've all known Connor since he was very little. He trusts them. I hate to think one of them would do this to him."

"But from what you tell me," Roger said, "this couldn't be accidental."

"No, I'm sure it's not." Joy curled up on her side and rested her head on the arm of the couch.

"Have you ever heard of Munchausen syndrome by proxy?" Roger asked quietly.

Joy felt a sudden weight in her stomach. Yes, she had heard of it, a tragic mental illness, where a caregiver, usually a mother with a dependent child, makes up or causes various medical problems for the person being cared for. Sometimes the victim is subjected to painful tests and needless medical procedures because the caregiver craves attention from friends, family, and the medical staff he or she comes in contact with.

"I can't say that hasn't occurred to me in this case," she admitted. "I hadn't gone so far as calling it exactly that, but I've wondered about Veronica."

"You said Connor's been sickly all his life. His sister's moved away, and his father's dead?"

"Yes. And I know his mother doesn't want to lose him. But I don't know if she would go as far as hurting him to keep him close. She's definitely overprotective and clingy, but I haven't seen any sign of her actually doing anything that would keep him in the hospital. And he doesn't seem to have any sign of being abused like that, but…"

"But?"

Joy sighed. "But I can't absolutely rule her out. And I'm sure the police are very familiar with the syndrome, so they'll be investigating that too."

"How about the other two? The doctor and the filmmaker?"

"They both would like Connor to stay around so they can finish their projects, but they both seem to understand that he's growing up and wanting more control of his own life." She thought for a moment. "They don't seem like they'd hurt Connor either."

"But that's kind of the point, isn't it? Whoever's been doing this hasn't actually hurt him. I realize it's been scary for him, allergic reactions like the kind he's had always are, but it looks to me like your perpetrator knows exactly how far to go without causing him any actual damage."

"Someone with medical knowledge," Joy said grimly. "I think that's got to be the case. But that's not really helpful either. I think Swarna's the only one who doesn't have some kind of medical training."

"Even Daisy?"

"Daisy at least knows how to use a syringe. Her mother's diabetic."

"And what about Swarna. Are you sure she doesn't have some kind of medical background?"

"She said she doesn't."

Joy could almost see the dubious look on Roger's face. "But are you sure?"

"I don't know how I'd find that out."

"There can't be a lot of Swarna LeFryes out there on the internet. Maybe just do a search."

She chuckled. "Fair enough. I could do that. Her website did mention that she had gone to Africa when she was in high school. I guess I could see what I could find out about that to start with."

"It's worth a try. Did she go to school here in Charleston?"

"She didn't say specifically, but I get the impression that she's lived here most of her life. When she's not out globe-trotting, that is."

"Well, see what you can find, but try not to worry too much. The police are on the job too."

"You're right, but I won't stop looking into it. I don't want anything to happen to Connor."

"Let me know if there's anything I can do to help."

"You already have," Joy said. "I think going out on that walking tour was the best thing I could have done this weekend."

"I'm glad. We'll have to find more things to do like that. I had a great time too." Roger paused for a moment. "I had a great time with you."

"You made it a very special day. And thanks for encouraging me to finalize the party plans. I was letting it overwhelm me."

"You just needed to remember that you're not in this alone. You have lots of friends standing with you."

They talked for a few minutes more until he finally said he had to go.

"Everything's set for tomorrow night," he said, "and I'll make sure the cake is there on time and be there to see that everybody's ready to surprise Shirley."

"Thanks. I'll see you tomorrow night."

She was smiling when she ended the call. He was right. She wasn't alone. She didn't have to do everything on her own. She had a family, some by blood, some only through love and friendship.

Almost immediately her phone rang again. It was Anne and Evelyn on a conference call.

"What's up?" Joy asked them.

"I have something to tell you about," Evelyn said.

"This sounds serious," Joy said. "Go ahead."

Evelyn hesitated. "I think it might be a big deal, but it's interesting if nothing else."

"Oh yeah?"

"I found out what Dr. Dahlman was looking for in the records Dr. Morton requested for him."

"Really?" Joy asked. "How'd you do that?"

"Last time I turned records over to him, I asked him. They're all at least fifty years old, due to the HIPAA laws, so it wasn't an invasion of any patient's privacy."

"And?" Anne pressed. "Joy's on the phone now, so don't make me wait any longer."

"And he was checking into how allergies affected patients during their early years as opposed to their adult years," Evelyn said.

Joy caught her breath. Allergies. Both times, Connor had had an allergic reaction to something that had been given to him. Was this more than just an attempt at keeping the boy available for more testing? Was this a part of the testing itself?

"Oh," she breathed finally. "Oh my."

"So it's probably a big deal."

"It certainly looks like a big deal to me," Joy said. "Why didn't you tell me before now?"

"I got home only a little while ago, and I didn't want to call you from work. I realize the records are old, but it still looks bad for me to be discussing patient records with someone who's not a doctor."

"True. Okay, after we're through here, I'll call Rebekah and let her know what you said. I'm sure she'll want to talk to you. Are you okay with that?"

"Sure. I don't want Dr. Morton or Dr. Dahlman mad at me, but I don't want anything to happen to Connor Sherman either."

"Actually, let me call Rebekah right now," Joy said. "I'll feel better if she knows, and she's the best one to take it from this point. I'll call you both back in a minute."

As she expected, Rebekah was very interested in the information Joy had gotten from Evelyn and what she had found out about

Daisy leaving Mr. Billingsly's room. She said she would follow up on all of it as soon as possible. Then, because the whole thing was making Joy uncomfortable, she called Veronica.

"Hi," Joy said. "I hope I'm not catching you at a bad time."

"Oh no. Connor's paying a video game, and I'm crocheting. Nothing much to do until Dr. Dahlman comes to start the sleep study."

Joy's heartbeat sped up a little.

"That's good," she said, stalling for a moment until she could think of the right thing to say. "Uh, have you heard anything new from the police?"

Rebekah wouldn't have had time to contact Veronica about this new information yet, and she probably wouldn't until she had done some investigation about it.

"No," Veronica said, "but I suppose they have a lot of other cases to work on too."

"True. Well, I only wanted to check on you. Make sure you keep an eye on things there. Nobody's going to try anything if you're always watching."

"I certainly will be. I might not look like much, but I can get real mean if somebody's after one of my cubs."

Joy chuckled. "I'm sure. Oh, tell me something. I was looking on Swarna's website, but there's not much on there about her personally. I'm curious though. Has she ever talked about where she was raised or her family or her early life?"

"Not very much," Veronica said. "I know she went to high school in a little place called Aurora, Nebraska, about twenty years ago, but that's really all she's ever mentioned to me. She says she's a citizen of the world now."

"That sounds like Swarna, from what I've seen of her. Well, I have to make some phone calls, so I'd better go. I'll check with you in the morning before you and Connor leave the hospital, okay?"

"That would be great. And I still hope we can get together for coffee sometime. Just as neighbors."

"And friends," Joy said.

"And friends. Thank you, Joy. I'll see you tomorrow."

Joy ended the call with mixed feelings. She still couldn't rule out Veronica being the one who was trying to harm Connor. But if it was actually Dr. Dahlman, and he was the one who would have access to Connor during the sleep study, at least Veronica would be on guard. Joy couldn't ignore what Evelyn had just told her, even if it was only a coincidence.

She dialed Evelyn and Anne back right away.

"I called Veronica after I talked to Rebekah. She and Connor are waiting for Dr. Dahlman. Sounds like things are pretty quiet there."

"Did you tell her about Dr. Dahlman?" Evelyn asked.

"I didn't mention any names at this point. We don't have any evidence that he's actually done anything wrong. I did make sure she was going to stay with Connor all the time. And I told Rebekah about what you found out. She's the actual detective after all."

"I feel better about it now," Anne said. "I don't want anything else to happen to that poor boy."

"I hope it won't," Joy told her, but she couldn't help the heaviness that wouldn't leave the pit of her stomach. "I'm going to do some research on Swarna LeFrye."

"Have you found out anything new on her?" Evelyn asked.

"Not particularly. Her website is very vague about her personally, but Veronica told me where she went to school, so I'm hoping to find out more about her from that. Could be there's a yearbook online with her in it. That might give us some ideas about what she was interested in back then."

"Well, let us know if you find out anything interesting," Anne said.

"I'm going to try to verify what Swarna told me," Joy assured her, "and that's what I want to do. Or at the least I want to find out more about her. Connor's mother told me where Swarna went to school, so maybe I can track her down that way."

"Good luck then," Anne said.

"And let me know if we can help you out with that too," Evelyn added.

"Thanks," Joy said. "I will."

She hung up and immediately went to her computer to look up Aurora High School.

"The Huskies," she murmured as she looked over their website, but of course there wouldn't be any information about students from twenty years ago.

She found one of those online yearbook sites and searched for "Swarna LeFrye," and then "LeFrye" by itself, and then just "Swarna." No luck. Could she have changed her name? It was certainly possible. In fact, it seemed very likely that someone like her would want an unusual and memorable "stage name." But, besides poring over every yearbook from Aurora High School for a period of ten or more years to try to be sure of finding her, what could Joy do now?

She considered for a moment. Swarna's website had mentioned a missionary trip to Africa. Maybe that was in connection with the school. If not, maybe there was an article about the trip in the local paper that mentioned the school. It wouldn't hurt to try a search. Aurora was a small town after all, and something like that had to have been big news.

She searched for "trip to Africa Aurora high school Nebraska." There were several articles about the high school, most often about the football team, and about the town, but none of them mentioned any trips to Africa. Finally, though, Joy found one that looked like a good possibility.

It was actually a post on a Facebook page from a man who had gone to Aurora High School and had traveled with some of his classmates nineteen years earlier as part of a medical missionary group to Nigeria. The post mentioned how much going to that part of the world had changed him and how grateful he felt to be living where he lived and how much it made him appreciate volunteers who traveled to other countries, and to the struggling parts of America, to help those with little or nothing.

There were several pictures that went with the post, and Joy smiled to see how very young and how very earnest the students looked. Then she caught her breath. There were several students handing out food and water to a line of Nigerian children and their parents. Two of them were helping an older man and woman give vaccinations. One of these students was a girl with abundant brown hair and smoky green eyes. She was smiling at the child she was vaccinating, and Joy recognized that smile, despite the two decades that separated it from the smile she had seen.

It was Swarna.

Chapter Seventeen

Joy scanned the caption. Judging by the order of the names, this girl was named Lisa Franklin. Definitely a more commonplace name than Swarna LeFrye. Joy looked at the girl in the picture again and then she switched to Swarna's website, to the picture that was taken about halfway between the present and when Lisa Franklin had gone to Africa as a medical missionary. Even with the hair not permed, the resemblance between the two photos was striking.

Lisa Franklin was Swarna LeFrye.

Joy looked at what was listed under Lisa Franklin's photo in the yearbook. Interests: photography, film, literature, travel, exploring the unknown. That certainly fit Swarna. She searched for what she could find under "Lisa Franklin Aurora Nebraska." There was very little there. She had won a prize for a photograph she had taken of a wrecked car when she was a high school freshman. She had gone to a poetry competition the next year, but there was no record of whether or not she had won anything. She was listed as an Aurora Huskie graduate two years later. That was all.

"*Sometimes I wish I had even a little experience in medicine,*" Swarna had said.

Joy wasn't sure if her visit to Nigeria made her statement untrue. Did giving a few vaccines in primitive conditions really count as medical experience? Swarna—Lisa—had been very young at the time of that trip. Maybe the experience had never even entered her mind when she'd made the comment.

There was nothing Joy could do but call Rebekah Osborne at the police department and let her know what she'd found out. Rebekah sounded distracted and rushed—no doubt she had a number of cases to juggle—but she was grateful for the information and said she would follow up on it when she interviewed Swarna and the others the next afternoon.

That would have to do.

Joy got to work very early as usual on Tuesday morning. Before she went to the gift shop, she decided to go up to Connor's room and see how things were going. She didn't want to wake anyone, but at least she could check with the nurses' station to make sure nothing unusual had happened during the night.

The nurse on duty gave her a brilliant smile and a cheerful good morning.

"You must be one of my fellow early birds," Joy said. "How are things going?"

"Pretty quiet, actually," the nurse said.

"How's Connor doing?"

"Not a peep. I checked on him about an hour ago. He and his mom were both asleep. I expect Dr. Dahlman to come back before too much longer and check on his sleep study. And I imagine Dr. Morton will be in later to examine Connor and then let us send him home."

"That's great news. Well, I'm going to get to work. If you get a chance, please tell Veronica that I'll be up to see her and Connor when my assistant comes to take over for me."

"Will do," the nurse said.

Joy felt a hundred pounds lighter as she headed down to the gift shop. No, she hadn't figured out what was going on with Connor yet, but she had done what she could to help the police, Rebekah planned to interview the suspects this afternoon, and nothing had happened to Connor overnight. Soon, she hoped, Connor would be at home and out of harm's way.

When Joy got to the shop, Shirley stood at the door, her arms folded across her chest.

"About time," she said, her lips pursed in pretend displeasure.

"Another early bird. Happy birthday!"

"Thanks."

Joy unlocked the door, and Shirley followed her inside.

"Coffee?" Joy asked.

"I'd love some." Shirley sank heavily into a chair at the back room table. "This getting old isn't for sissies."

Joy chuckled as she started the coffee. "You're only a baby at this point. Wait till you get to be my age."

"As they say, it's not the age, it's the mileage. I think I've been on my feet for ten hours straight. I haven't had a break all night till now."

"Sounds like you deserve one. How's it going otherwise?"

Shirley shrugged. "Okay. I could use another weekend."

"You never told me how it went at the jazz concert. Did you have fun?"

"It was great. Garrison…" Shirley's eyes warmed. "I could get used to having that man around all the time."

"He sure is nice. I hope you two get to go out more."

"I'd like that. The concert was a wonderful birthday present. And I'm excited about our dinner party too. We are still meeting for dinner tonight, right?"

"Of course we are. We've been looking forward to it. And we're not meeting. We're picking you up."

"And I guess you still won't tell me where we're going or anything."

"Nope," Joy said smugly.

"Or what to wear? I never ended up buying any of those outfits I was looking at."

"Wear something festive but comfortable. How's that?"

"Festive?"

"Festive. It's your night, remember?"

"Now you're making me nervous. And Anne and Evelyn won't tell me anything either."

"Good. They're not supposed to."

"But every time I go talk to them, they shut up and look guilty."

"Perfect. Now you need to mind your own business and let us mind ours." She got up, poured them each a cup of piping hot coffee, and brought the cups back to the table. "All you need to do is be ready when we come to pick you up and then enjoy what we have planned."

"Are you telling her all our secrets?" Evelyn asked as she and Anne came into the shop.

"I'm trying to get her to," Shirley said. "No luck so far."

"Happy birthday," Anne said.

She was quickly echoed by Evelyn, and they both gave Shirley a hug. Then they helped themselves to coffee too and sat down at the table.

"Do you have everything set with your mom for the evening?" Anne asked with complete innocence.

"Dot's coming to keep her company," Shirley told her. "They'll have a nice, quiet night together. I was telling Joy that I'm looking forward to our dinner. It'll be a cozy meal with lots of girl talk."

Joy widened her eyes out of Shirley's sight, already second-guessing her party plans. Evelyn caught her glance and smiled slyly, assuring her that Shirley would love the surprise party with delicious food and good friends, even if it wasn't what she was expecting.

"We're not confirming or denying anything," Evelyn said smoothly. "Only that we're getting together tonight, and we'll pick you up at seven."

Shirley grinned. "I'm excited."

"So are we," Anne said.

Shirley took a drink of her coffee. "Now tell me what's happening with your neighbor, the boy genius."

"Oh, I've been needing to catch you up on that," Joy said.

She didn't mention that, during their talks about the party, she had already discussed everything about Connor with Anne and Evelyn. That was all right though. It would help her organize her thoughts if she could go through everything she had found out over the past few days and see what the fresh eyes of her friends saw in it.

"Sounds like any of them could have done it," Shirley said once Joy had laid out all the evidence. "I don't know who to wonder about most."

"I'm sorry," Evelyn said, glancing around to make sure no one had come into the shop, "but I worry about the mother. I can't see somebody like Daisy going so far to do something like this. The doctor and the filmmaker, they're professionals. Sure, they want Connor to stay around so they can finish the projects they've been working on for so long, but they have to realize they'd lose everything, especially their professional reputations, if they did anything underhanded. Especially something involving a minor, which Connor still is."

"That's true," Joy admitted.

"I'd have to look at the mother, if I were investigating the case. She's a little too needy if you ask me."

"But she's his mother," Anne said, wincing.

"And sometimes, as awful as its sounds, it happens," Evelyn said.

"True," Joy admitted, "but she hasn't shown any sign of doing anything."

"Unless she's behind what's been going on here lately."

"She wasn't here when Connor ate that candy, but she was there when Swarna first brought it. She left before Swarna did, but that doesn't mean she couldn't have come back while everybody was out. Still, wouldn't she have a history of doing this, if she really is behind it all? Connor's been filmed and studied since he was a baby.

Wouldn't Swarna or one of the doctors have noticed something before now?"

"Maybe she just started," Evelyn suggested.

"But something would have had to set her off, wouldn't it?" Shirley asked.

"Maybe." Joy considered for a moment. "Her daughter went to college this year, so for the first time, she has Connor and nobody else. Does that kind of situation trigger a Munchausen-type reaction? I'd have to see what I can find out."

"Don't forget Daisy," Anne said, and then she raised one hand before the others could protest. "I'm not saying it is Daisy, but I think you underestimate what she might be capable of. Didn't you say she would have been valedictorian if Connor hadn't been around?"

"Yes."

"So she's smart. She doesn't have the money to go to school if she doesn't get some kind of scholarship or grant, and Connor's probably going to beat her out of the one given to the class valedictorian. Did you ever find out if that's her handwriting on the card that came with Connor's flowers?"

"I didn't think to ask Rebekah about that, but I imagine she's had that handwriting analyzed by now. Maybe she'll have some information when she comes to talk to everybody this afternoon."

"Whatever's going on," Shirley said, "you've told the police everything you know. They can handle it from here. You've done what you can."

"Yeah," Joy said on a sigh. "I know you're right. But I want to make sure Connor's all right, and I won't feel comfortable about him until he's out of the hospital."

"Unless it really is his mom," Anne said.

"That would be awful."

"Maybe you should go check on him, Joy," Shirley said, "if it'll make you feel better."

"Oh, I did. First thing." Joy gave her a mischievous grin. "I checked with the nurse when I got in this morning. She said Connor had a good night with no problems."

"There you go," Evelyn said. "So relax and have a good day. And think about how much fun we're going to have tonight."

"Yeah, I'm eager to go," Shirley said. "I love eating at, um, what's the name of that place again?"

"Oh no," Joy told her, laughing. "It's a surprise. Festive and comfortable, that's all you get to know at this point."

Shirley laughed too. "All right. I'll be patient." She glanced at her watch. "I'd better get home and get some sleep, or I will end up snoring right through my birthday."

She stood up and so did everyone else.

"Get some rest," Anne said, giving her a hug. "And we'll see you tonight."

Evelyn hugged her too. "We're going to have so much fun."

"Yes, we are," Joy said, adding her own hug. "So be ready by seven, and we'll come get you."

"Definitely," Shirley said. "I'll see all of you later on."

She walked out of the gift shop, and the remaining three moved conspiratorially closer to each other.

"Is there anything else we need to do before tonight?" Anne asked.

"I don't think so," Joy said. "Have you invited everybody?"

"Yes. Everybody's on board."

"And so have I," Evelyn said. "And yes, they're all coming."

"All right," Joy said. "I'm going to call Hannibal's and make sure they're going to be ready for us. And I'll call Roger to check on the cake, though I suppose he has that all taken care of. I want to remind Dot to have Regina ready to go."

"What are they going to do?" Evelyn asked. "If Regina is dressed to go out, Shirley is going to want to know why. And if Regina and Dot leave the house before Shirley does, she's really going to wonder what's going on."

"No, no," Joy assured her. "Dot is going to tell Shirley she and Regina are going for a drive and then to get something to eat. And it'll be true."

Evelyn snickered. "Neatly done."

"So we're set," Anne said. "I'd better remind Ralph so he doesn't get distracted and forget to come home on time."

"Do you want me to pick you both up?" Joy asked. "Or how do we want to do this?"

"Why don't you let me drive?" Anne asked. "You've been great about taking care of almost everything. You shouldn't have to drive too."

Joy felt a touch of warmth inside her heart, glad to be appreciated. "All right. I'd like that. Pick me up a little before seven. We'll pick up Shirley and then head over to Hannibal's. Everybody ought to be there before we are."

"We told them to try to get there a little early if they can," Evelyn said. "They don't have to stay the whole evening if they don't want to, but we want a nice group there to say surprise."

"Perfect. I'll be ready when you get to my house. I have a feeling that it's going to be a long, slow day until then."

Anne finished her coffee and then put all the cups on the counter next to the coffee maker. "You can make your phone calls. That ought to pass some of the time."

"We'll see you tonight, if we don't see you around," Evelyn added, and she and Anne headed out to the lobby.

Fortunately for Joy, the morning actually passed quickly. Hannibal's had everything in the works for the party, Dot hadn't forgotten about their plans for that evening, and Roger had arranged for Andre to meet him at Hannibal's at about six thirty in order to set up the cake.

"I figured somebody ought to be there to keep everything in order, especially when the guests start to arrive. Are you going to let us know when you've almost got Shirley to the restaurant? I want to make sure everybody keeps quiet until she opens the door to the party room."

"I hadn't thought about that. Uh…how about if I text you when we pull into the parking lot? Anne's driving, so I'll sit in the back seat, behind Shirley, and she'll never notice."

"Great plan." Roger chuckled. "I'm enjoying our little caper. I think Shirley will too."

"I hope so. She still thinks it's going to be only the four of us, so I know she'll be surprised."

"And how are things going with your neighbor today? Is the boy still in the hospital?"

"I went to check on him earlier. It sounds like he's fine. I'm pretty sure he'll go home today."

"Good. I hope that's the end to whatever was going on."

"I'll feel better when somebody figures out what happened and why. I don't like only wondering, which is what I'm doing at this point. But a detective is supposed to question the people around Connor, and maybe she'll figure it out."

"Or scare away the perp," Roger said.

"Maybe so. Anyway, I'd better get to work for now. I'm looking forward to tonight."

"It's going to be fun," he told her, "and I think you're going to love the cake."

"Thanks for taking care of it for me. With you and the girls helping, I think we got it all done."

"And all you have to do tonight is relax and enjoy yourself, okay?"

"Yes," she said. "Exactly. See you in a little while, and please thank Andre for me."

"Will do. See you soon."

Joy stayed busy most of the morning, and it passed swiftly. Daisy stopped by before lunchtime just to say hi.

"I'm going to see how Mr. Billingsly is. I hope he gets to leave today."

"He's such a nice man," Joy told her. "I talked with him for a few minutes yesterday. He's enjoyed spending time with you."

"I like him too. I think I'm going to ask if I can keep visiting him at his assisted living place. I want to at least finish reading *Curtain* with him. He's read it before, I know, but he won't tell me anything. He says I can work it out for myself."

"And have you?"

Daisy shrugged. "There's a lot going on, and I'm really not sure."

"Well, read on. The more clues you have, the better you'll do."

"Sometimes there are too many clues, and it looks like everybody is guilty."

Tell me about it, Joy thought.

"I understand Connor Sherman is going home today," she said, watching Daisy's expression. "Probably anyway."

"Is he?"

Daisy was obviously trying to look uninterested.

"I think so."

Daisy shrugged again. "I've been staying away. He doesn't want to talk to me, and his mom will think I'm trying to do something awful to him."

"Maybe you've got it all wrong about him," Joy said, the idea coming to her abruptly as she read disappointment behind the girl's nonchalance. "Didn't you say he and you used to be friends?"

"Kind of. We talked in school some."

"And when did he start avoiding you?"

"It was after we sat next to each other at the pep rally." She looked down at the floor. "A couple of the guys in our class, my age, said something to him. I don't know what it was, but they were kind of snickering to each other. And then Connor wouldn't talk to me anymore."

"What do you think they said?"

"I don't know. Probably what a loser I am."

"I hardly think that," Joy said. "You know, boys Connor's age, especially shy boys, might be all right with talking to a girl until he realizes he likes her."

Color flamed into Daisy's face. "I don't think it's that."

"Are you sure?"

"He's only a kid," Daisy muttered.

Joy remembered the look on Connor's face when he was talking about the florist's card he'd been using for a bookmark. Just a card, he had said. Just a card from whom?

"Did you ever send him flowers?" she asked.

Daisy caught a quick breath. "I'm telling the truth. Really. I didn't send him those daisies. I don't know how—"

"No, I don't mean those flowers. Did you ever send him flowers before now? Maybe last year or something?"

The color in Daisy's face deepened. "Please don't say anything. It would only make him mad."

"Then you did."

Daisy nodded.

"When was that?"

"It was this January. After Christmas break, he was sick and didn't come back to school with everybody else. I heard he was in the hospital, so I sent him some flowers. I didn't say they were from me or anything."

"And what did you write on the card?"

Joy was sure she already knew. She hoped she knew.

Daisy bit her lip. "Get well soon."

Chapter Eighteen

"Only 'Get well soon,'" Daisy added. "That was all I wrote on the card I sent."

Joy couldn't help smiling. "Nothing else?"

"No."

"Do you think Connor knows what your handwriting looks like?"

"I—I don't know. Maybe. We worked on some projects together last year. I gave him copies of my notes for a couple of classes when he was sick and couldn't come to school."

"Then he probably does. Do you know what happened to that card you sent with the flowers last year?"

Daisy shook her head.

"He's been using it for a bookmark for months now."

"Really?" Daisy's eyes lit. "You're not kidding?"

"That's what he told me. He wouldn't say much about it, but that's kind of a funny thing for a boy to hang on to if it didn't mean something to him."

"But—I mean—"

"Here's the other thing," Joy said, "and it's the important part right now. He doesn't have the card anymore. It's been missing since before those daisies were sent to him."

"You mean somebody took it?"

"I mean exactly that. Somebody took it, and that same somebody used it to copy your writing, just that particular phrase, so the card that came with the daisies would look as if it came from you."

"Wow," Daisy said. "Who would do that?"

"That's what we need to find out."

Daisy bit her lip, a pleased little smile touching the corners of her mouth. "And you really think Connor kept that card all this time because of me?"

"It seems that that's the only explanation that makes sense. But I'd have to leave it up to you to find out."

"But his mom—"

"Don't worry about his mom. We'll figure out who's behind all this, and then she won't think she has to suspect you."

The happiness Joy felt for the youngsters suddenly paled. If somehow Veronica was herself behind all this, Connor was going to have a lot more to deal with than getting his mother to like the girl he had a crush on.

"What's wrong?" Daisy asked.

Joy forced a slight smile. "Don't worry about it. The great news is that we have an explanation for why the handwriting on the card that came with the daisies looks so much like yours."

"Yeah. I kinda forgot that was the important part." Daisy glanced at the clock behind the counter. "Oh man, I have to run. I promised Mr. Billingsly I'd be by to see him before now. I hope they didn't already discharge him."

"You'd better hurry then."

Daisy gave Joy an impulsive hug. "Thank you, Joy. Really."

"You're welcome. Now you'd better get going."

Daisy hurried off as an elderly couple came into the shop looking for cough drops and lip balm. Joy located what they needed and then helped two teen boys find a card and a box of candy for their mother, who had that morning given birth to a baby girl. Lacy came in a few minutes after they left and, once they had both waited on a sudden influx of customers, Joy told Lacy she was going to take a break for a few minutes.

She went up the elevator to the second floor and straight to Connor's room. The door was open, and she peeked inside.

"Knock, knock."

"Come in," Veronica said cheerfully.

Joy found her standing at the counter next to the sink looking into an open carry-on bag.

"Mom was just making sure I get home with everything I brought," Connor said, grinning from ear to ear. "Now that we're finally going home."

"You got your walking papers," Joy said. "Congratulations."

"Yeah. From Dr. Dahlman and Dr. Morton. All that needs to happen now is that they need to get this IV out of my arm."

"Not quite," Veronica told him. "Dr. Morton said he wants you to get one more round of fluids before you go."

"Ugh." Connor flung himself back against his pillows. "I'm fine! I can drink water and stuff at home, can't I?"

"Not the same. Now calm down. It won't take that long. Another half hour or so."

"Or hour," Connor grumbled. "Or two. If the nurse shows up anytime soon."

"Now, not that long. Be patient."

"Mom."

"All right, I'll go and see if I can hurry things along," Veronica said. "How would that be?"

"Thanks, Mom."

"Would you please watch out for him till I get back?" she asked Joy.

"Nothing's going to happen," Connor insisted.

"All right. All right."

Veronica hurried out the door, and Connor rolled his eyes.

"I've got to get out of here."

Joy smiled at his eagerness and at the thought of Daisy's obvious interest in him, an interest she was almost certain was mutual. "How are you feeling today? How did your sleep study go?"

"It was okay," Connor said. "I never can sleep that great with all those wires on me, but it was all right. Dr. Dahlman won't have any results for a while, I guess, but he seemed pretty happy to get it done."

"I was." Dr. Dahlman came into the room, grinning broadly. "I'd like to keep you around for another week or two, but I guess that wouldn't be too practical, now would it?"

"Only if you want to do a study on guys going bonkers because they can't get out of the hospital," Connor told him seriously.

"I know. I know. Places to go, people to see. Well, I can't complain. You've put up with so much the past few days, and I'm proud of you. I know I'm going to get a lot out of what I've observed here."

"You've got to admit it," Veronica said as she came back into the room with a blanket in her arms. "You couldn't have found a better subject for your study."

"No," Dr. Dahlman said proudly. "Exactly the mental capacity I was looking for, the right age, and patient enough to put up with everything I've thrown at you all this time." He turned to Veronica. "And you have a very patient mother too."

"If my boy could help other people, I was happy to help that happen," Veronica said. "I like to think it's my little contribution, for what it's worth."

"It's been worth a great deal," the doctor assured her. "To me and countless other doctors and scientists who'll benefit from these studies."

"Is the nurse coming, Mom?" Connor asked.

"She said she'd be in here in just a minute. Why don't you let me put this blanket over you so you don't get a chill?"

"Ugh. I'm not going to get a chill, Mom."

"I'm sorry." Veronica put the blanket on an empty chair. "Anyway, she said she's coming."

"Okay. But I hope she hurries. I really want to get out of here."

"I suppose I'm going to have to make the most of whatever time I can get with Connor from now on," the doctor said.

"I suppose that makes two of us," Swarna said, coming into the room. "Looks like you're finally going to leave us."

"Finally," Connor said, looking slightly annoyed. "I might as well tell you all this while you're here. Mom, everybody, I've made a decision about what I'm going to do. I've been thinking about it a lot since I've been here, especially since I had to stay last night. I'm going to finish school this spring. I'll apply to MIT right away. Maybe they'll have some online courses or something I can start with in the summer.

Or maybe I can test out of some classes and get to the good stuff right away."

"Now, Connor," Veronica said, "you know you can't do any of that without my permission. You're too young yet."

"I'm not asking to go live in China or something, Mom. All I want is to go to school somewhere where I'm not bored out of my mind and doing a lot of busy work until I'm a year or two older. Why should I waste all that time I can never get back?"

"Because you're still fifteen! Honey, I know you're eager to start learning new things, but you're fifteen. You should enjoy this part of your life while you can."

"You mean spending my time being studied and filmed and being in and out of hospitals? That part of my life?"

"Connor," Veronica pled. "Honey, please. Can't we talk about this later?"

"Sure." Connor pressed his lips together for a moment, and then he looked her in the eye. "I know you can keep me from doing anything until I'm eighteen," he said. "But I won't like you for it."

"Hey, now," Dr. Dahlman said reasonably. "You two can work this out, okay? Cool down and talk about it when you get home. Your mom's right. Be a boy while you can. The other stuff will still be there."

"Do you think I'd be doing the wrong thing?" Connor asked him. "If I went to MIT or something as soon as possible?"

"For one thing, your mother is right. You're not even sixteen yet. That's awfully young to be on your own. College isn't like high school. You'd be around students who are a lot older than you in most cases, all of them on their own, mostly for the first time.

College students aren't always known for their exemplary behavior or good decision-making skills. It could be easy for you to get in over your head in a situation like that."

Connor frowned, but he looked as if he at least reluctantly recognized the possibility. "Well, Mom could move up there and keep an eye on me, couldn't she?"

"That would be up to her, but it would be a pretty big decision for her to make right now, don't you think? Even if you were accepted right this minute somewhere, you wouldn't get to start classes tomorrow. There would be a lot of details to take care of first, here and at the school. Why don't you take it easy for a little while and see what you and your mother can work out?"

Connor clenched his jaw. "Okay."

Dr. Dahlman patted his shoulder. "Don't be in such a hurry. You're going to be grown up a lot more years than you're going to be a boy."

"Yeah, and the longer I stay around, the longer you'll get to do your tests and stuff." Connor looked at Swarna. "And your filming."

"Only if you're all right with that," she told him good-naturedly. "I told you all along, you're the boss. I'd have liked something a little more dramatic to end the film with, but I think if we show you going off to conquer MIT, that would be a pretty satisfying ending."

Joy noticed the look Connor gave Dr. Dahlman at that, maybe not accusing, but certainly challenging. It was if he was saying that Swarna was ready to let him go and demanding to know if the doctor was willing to do the same.

"You know I want the best for you," Dr. Dahlman said. "I think MIT would be glad to have you. Someday. And it's not too early to start finding out if what they have to offer is what you really want. But try not to get in over your head. It's different when you're on your own. A little more time here wouldn't do you any harm."

"What will you do when Connor isn't around anymore?" Joy asked him.

"Honestly, I don't know. I wish I could keep him until he's about twenty-five, to be honest. The brain really isn't fully developed before then." Dr. Dahlman shook his head. "It would be a shame to cut off data at this point. But maybe he'll give me a little time now and then when he can so I can update my analysis."

The nurse came in before he could say anything else, and Veronica fussed over her son while the new IV bag was hooked up.

"I'll be back to check on you in a little while," the nurse said finally. "Dr. Morton says you ought to be able to go home when this bag's empty."

"Thanks," Connor said. "I'm ready."

"What about you, Swarna?" Joy asked when the nurse was gone.

"I guess I'll start editing what I have," Swarna said. "I've got hours of film from the past several years. Some of it's already edited, but it'll take months for me to put the rest together. I won't be bored."

Veronica sighed, and tears filled her eyes. "I can't let him go yet. Not yet."

"Mom," Connor grumbled, scratching his arm distractedly. "Not in front of everybody, okay? Come on."

"Well, I'm sorry." She dabbed her eyes with a tissue. "But what if something happened to you?"

There was a moment of taut silence.

"I suppose I'd better get back to work then," Joy said.

"I have to go too," Dr. Dahlman said, glancing at his watch. "I have a conference call to make. Connor, I hope you'll consider staying to finish your high school year here at least. But I'd be glad to see you at MIT. Someday."

"Thanks," Connor said, making no promises.

"And I'm supposed to judge some experimental films for one of the community colleges," Swarna told him, "so I probably should head that way." She smiled wryly. "If you decide to do something dramatic, give me a call first, okay? I always have my camera ready to go."

Connor rubbed the side of his neck. "I think I'll take a hard pass on any more drama. Thanks anyway."

"Come on," Joy said. "I'll walk with you two to the elevator. Swarna, I would really like to see your film on Connor when you're finished with it."

Veronica followed them all out into the hallway. "I'm sure it will be wonderful," she gushed, "and I'm sure Connor isn't serious about not doing any more filming. He's going through a phase right now. Boys his age can be very changeable."

"I think he'll stay," Dr. Dahlman said. "He's trying to see how much independence he can get right now, but I'm sure he'll realize that he's not quite ready to really be on his own."

They'd reached the elevators, but Veronica clutched the doctor's arm before he could push the button.

"Somebody has to make him see sense," she said. "He's not ready. I wish I could make him understand that."

"Don't you worry." Dr. Dahlman patted her hand and then moved it from his arm so he could push the button to summon the elevator. "I don't think he'll do anything rash."

The doors opened, and Veronica got on the elevator with the rest of them, still talking. "You know he's got a stubborn streak when he wants to do something."

The doctor chuckled. "I'm well aware. But really, I simply don't think anything is going to come of this right now."

"I think he's trying to let us all know what he's planning to do," Swarna said as the elevator started down. "To get us used to the idea ahead of time."

"I don't know." Veronica sighed. "At this point I'd rather he had to stay in the hospital for a while longer so he wouldn't be in such a hurry to leave home."

That would be the perfect way to make him even more eager to be on his own.

"You have to let them go sometime," Joy said.

"He's too young yet," Veronica said, her voice unsteady. "He's too young."

"There's no need to be upset at this point." Dr. Dahlman put his arm around her shoulders. "You'll work things out with him, and I don't think he's going anywhere. Not for a while yet."

"All I want is to keep him safe."

The elevator stopped, the doors opened to the lobby, and they all got out.

"I'm sorry." Veronica wiped her eyes with one hand and smiled sheepishly. "I'm sure you're right and Connor and I will figure this out."

"You will," he assured her.

"Well, I'd better get back up there. He's eager to get home, and I want to have all of our things ready to go when Dr. Morton releases him. We'll stay in touch with you, Doctor. And you, Swarna. Joy, we really need to meet for coffee soon."

"Anytime," Joy told her.

"Soon," Veronica said, and she pressed the button for the elevator.

The door opened almost immediately. A wild-eyed Daisy was standing there.

"Mrs. Sherman, you've got to come back. It's Connor. He's having trouble breathing."

Chapter Nineteen

VERONICA PUT BOTH HANDS OVER her heart. "What? What happened? Oh, let me in there."

Joy, Swarna, and Dr. Dahlman followed her back onto the elevator.

"Tell me what happened," Veronica demanded as the doors closed again. "What did you do?"

"I didn't do anything," Daisy insisted. "I didn't even see him. I was going to visit Mr. Billingsly, and Connor's nurse told me to hurry and see if I could catch you. She said he was having breathing problems, but she didn't say why."

"Another allergic reaction?" Dr. Dahlman asked. "Have they called Morton?"

"I don't know," Daisy admitted. "The nurse just told me to hurry and get his mom before she left."

"I was coming right back," Veronica said. "Oh, I should have stayed there. I knew he wasn't safe on his own. I thought being gone only a minute or two wouldn't hurt anything."

Joy put a steadying hand on her shoulder. "I'm sure Dr. Morton is on his way."

"If it's like before," Swarna said, "it won't be too bad. He'll be all right."

Veronica bolted out of the elevator the instant the doors opened. The nurse was waiting outside Connor's door.

"Dr. Morton is already in there," she said. "He wants everyone to wait out here. Maybe you could go to the waiting room until he has some news for you."

"But what's wrong?" Veronica wailed. "What did he say?"

"He's not sure yet. He thinks it's something he's allergic to again. He's already given him something. Please, it would be better if all of you went in the waiting room until the doctor can come talk to you."

"Who was it?" Veronica grabbed the nurse's upper arms. "Who was in there with him?"

"Nobody."

"It wasn't Daisy?"

"I didn't—" Daisy began.

"No," the nurse said. "Nobody was in there. Daisy was coming down the hall when I realized Connor was having trouble, so I asked her to find you. That's all."

"But he was fine when we left. I hadn't left him alone since what happened with the candy. Not till now."

"Come on," Dr. Dahlman soothed. "Let's sit down for a moment and see what Dr. Morton says."

"But tell me what happened," Veronica begged the nurse.

"Let's go into the waiting room," the doctor said, leading her that way. "We can talk about it."

"I was at my desk," the nurse said once everyone had sat down in the waiting room. "Connor pressed the call button, and I went in there. He had red welts on his neck and arms, and his face was starting to swell. I could tell he could hardly breathe, so I called

Dr. Morton right away. He gave Connor an antihistamine and then asked me to wait for you to come back upstairs and tell you what happened."

Veronica's hands were twisted together in her lap. "How bad is it?"

"You'll have to let the doctor give you the details. That's all I really know. He's got his own nurse in there with him."

"I'm sure Connor will be all right," Swarna soothed. "He's been through this before."

"But why?" Veronica asked, tears spilling down her pale cheeks. "Why is somebody doing this to him?"

"Maybe it was nothing more than a mistake. Something in his medication?"

"But he wasn't taking anything. The only thing he had was—" Veronica caught her breath. "Oh, Connor!"

Joy looked up to see an orderly wheeling Connor's bed into the hallway. Dr. Morton was walking alongside it."

Veronica leaped up and ran to the waiting room door.

"Dr. Morton," she cried as she flung the door open. "What's going on? What happened?"

"We're finding that out right now," he told her. "I think we've taken care of the worst of it."

"But what happened?"

"Did somebody bring him something to eat?" Dr. Morton asked her. "Lotion? Room spray? Anything at all?"

"No, nothing. He ate breakfast, but that was a few hours ago. He was fine."

"All right. We'll figure it out."

"Oh, Connor," she whispered, stroking her son's mottled cheek.

"We've got to get some tests run now," Dr. Morton said. "I'll be back to talk to you as soon as I can." He nodded at the orderly. "Let's go."

A moment later Connor was gone.

"Come on," Joy said gently. "The doctor will be back in a little while. Why don't you sit down and have some coffee?"

"That's a good idea," Dr. Dahlman said. "Come on."

"What about your conference call?" Veronica asked, sniffling.

"Let me contact them and postpone that for now," he said. "Give me a couple of minutes."

He took his phone from his pocket and walked to the end of the hall.

Joy took Veronica back into the waiting room and poured her a cup of coffee from the pot on the corner table. Swarna came and got herself some too.

"Are you going to be all right for now, Mrs. Sherman?" the nurse asked when her pager beeped.

"Yes, I think so," Veronica said. "You'd better go take care of whatever that is."

"I'll come check on you when I can. Try not to worry too much. I'm sure Dr. Morton will make sure Connor is all right."

"Thank you."

The nurse hurried out of the room, and Joy poured her own cup of coffee. Several minutes later the nurse returned.

"Have you heard from Dr. Morton yet?" Veronica asked immediately.

"Not yet," the nurse said. "I only wanted to make sure you didn't need anything."

"Nothing. Just some news."

"I'll let you know as soon as I hear something," the nurse said. "I'll be at the desk if you need me."

Joy watched her walk away, thinking about what Veronica had been saying a few minutes before. Connor hadn't had any medication before his reaction. What had she been about to say next? The only thing he had was what? The only thing Joy knew of was that new IV.

"I'll be right back," she said suddenly, and she went out to the nurse's station.

"Is everything all right?" Camilla, the nurse on duty, asked, and a couple of her fellow nurses looked up questioningly.

"Do you have a minute to talk?" Joy asked her. "This could be very important."

"Sure. What is it?"

Joy glanced at the other nurses and then nodded toward the break room across the hallway. "Could we speak privately?"

"All right." Camilla turned to the other two. "Hold down the fort for me. I'll be right back."

Joy and the nurse walked over to the break room.

"It looks like Connor had another allergic reaction, doesn't it?" Joy said.

Camilla nodded. "I don't know what might have triggered it though. He was fine after breakfast. Nobody was in his room except his mother, and she's well aware of what he's allergic to."

Joy felt that heaviness in her stomach again. With Connor, it seemed as if it didn't take much for something he ate to affect him. And yes, his mother knew that very well. If she actually was behind all this, it certainly wasn't a good idea for Connor to go home with her at this point. Still, he had seemed fine when Joy first came into his room.

"I'm wondering about the IV you gave him," Joy said. "It wasn't very long after that that Connor started reacting. It was the last thing he was given. What was in it?"

"Nothing," Camilla said. "It wasn't any kind of medication. Only fluids like the doctor ordered. I got it from supply myself."

"Could anyone have tampered with it?" Joy asked.

Camilla frowned. "I don't think so. It was on the counter at the desk, but I was there the whole time."

"Did anybody come by? To talk to you?"

"Well, yes. People come by there all the time. A couple of other nurses were at the desk off and on."

"Anybody specifically associated with Connor?"

"Well, Ms. LeFrye stopped to ask how Connor was doing before she went into his room, and before that Dr. Dahlman asked me if I knew whether Dr. Morton was coming to see Connor. Daisy, the volunteer, was here. Neither of them was there very long though."

I wish she could answer all the questions I have about this messed-up situation, Joy thought as Camilla gave her a few more details about what had happened while Connor's IV was at her desk. *I still have so many.*

Chapter Twenty

After she got through talking to Camilla, Joy stopped to call Detective Rebekah Osborne to tell her what was going on with Connor. Assured that Connor was getting urgent medical treatment, Rebekah said she would be out to the hospital to ask questions as soon as possible. She also said she would contact Dr. Morton to arrange for him to keep Connor away from any visitors until the police could make sure the boy was safe.

At least Camilla helped me eliminate one suspect, Joy thought as she went back into the waiting room where Daisy, Swarna, Dr. Dahlman, and Veronica were still expecting news.

"Did you find out anything?" Veronica asked at once.

"Nothing from Dr. Morton yet," Joy said. "But I was talking to Camilla about what might have happened to Connor."

Daisy sat up a little more in her chair.

"What did she say?" Swarna asked.

"We discussed whether Connor could have reacted to something in his IV," Joy told them.

"That's what I was thinking must have happened," Dr. Dahlman said. "He didn't eat or drink or touch anything he's allergic to when we were in the room, and he didn't have any reaction until after the IV was changed. The reaction time also indicates the IV was the instigator."

"But it couldn't have been the IV," Swarna said. "We all saw the nurse give it to Connor. Nobody was even near it after that."

"But they were near it before she brought it in," Joy said, looking at each of them in turn.

"You were there." Swarna nodded toward Daisy. "Why was that?"

Daisy's cheeks reddened. "Somebody called me and asked me to come there. I was supposed to take some flowers to one of the patients because they'd been taken to the wrong room, but when I got there, nobody knew what I was talking about."

"Who told you to come get the flowers?" Joy asked her.

"One of the nurses. She said her name was Mary and I was supposed to go to the nurse's station on the second floor, but Camilla said they don't have anybody named Mary. Not on this floor anyway."

"How did you know Daisy was there?" Joy asked Swarna.

"I stopped by the desk to see how Connor was doing. It was right before I went to his room."

"Did you see Daisy tamper with the IV?"

"No."

"And you could see the bag the whole time you were there?"

"Well, not the whole time," Swarna admitted. "I had a cramp in my calf while I was standing there, and I nearly fell over. I bent down to massage it, but it lasted only a few seconds. The nurse helped me stay upright. She said I need to take more magnesium, and I know I don't get nearly enough. I had another cramp while I was still standing there, and she was nice enough to get me a packet of mustard from the break room across the hall. That stopped it right away."

"That's an old trick," Dr. Dahlman said, "but it usually works."

"Was Daisy still at the desk when you got back?" Joy asked as Daisy looked at her pleadingly.

"I don't think so," Swarna said.

"I went to see what I ought to do about those flowers," Daisy said. "Ms. Kingston didn't know anything about them either, so I went back to tell Connor goodbye."

"You knew he was supposed to be leaving the hospital today?"

"That's what Camilla and Swarna were talking about when I came up to the desk. I'm sorry, Mrs. Sherman, I know you don't want me around, but I wanted to see how he was before he left."

Veronica looked at her warily and said nothing.

"And I understand you were there too," Joy told Dr. Dahlman. "Why was that?"

"I was looking for Dr. Morton," Dr. Dahlman said. "I wanted to find out if he was discharging Connor, and I was there for only a minute or two."

"Camilla told me you accidentally knocked a stack of files off the edge of the desk when you were there."

The doctor chuckled. "I'm afraid I did. And a cup full of pens. We managed to get them all back in order though."

"So all three of them could have put something in that IV that Connor's allergic to," Veronica said, her cheeks patched with red.

Daisy, Swarna, and Dr. Dahlman began to protest all at once.

"They could have," Veronica said stiffly, "but they didn't. I did."

Daisy gasped.

Joy stared at Veronica, startled. She couldn't be the one, the nurse had been certain of that. According to Camilla, Veronica got that blanket for Connor and never even came close to the IV.

Just as Joy was opening her mouth to protest, Veronica shot her a look, subtle but firm, and Joy snapped her mouth shut again. Veronica was up to something.

"I'm sorry," Veronica whispered, blotting her eyes with an already sodden tissue. "I'm sorry. I just couldn't let him go."

She sank into a chair and bowed her head, sobbing.

"What are you saying?" Joy asked her, trying to keep from looking utterly confused.

"I didn't want Connor to move out. He's only a baby still. I didn't want him to go away and leave me alone. He's not ready. I'm not ready!" Veronica's breathing hitched jerkily. "I thought if I could keep him in the hospital a little bit longer, he'd see that he's not well enough to be on his own yet. He's been getting better and better for several months now. Dr. Morton says he's outgrowing most of what's been bothering him since he was a baby, and he ought to be perfectly healthy soon."

"What did you do?" Dr. Dahlman demanded. "What did you give him? Dr. Morton should know right away."

"Just penicillin. Only a little bit. I know how allergic he is. He can't take very much without having a serious reaction, but I was careful. I gave him no more than a tiny bit. Only enough to keep him here another night. I wouldn't really hurt him, and I know even a little bit too much could kill him. I was really careful. I didn't want to hurt him. Not really."

"You gave him penicillin?" Swarna gasped.

Veronica nodded and buried her face in her hands, still sobbing. "I'm so sorry, but it was only a little."

"Oh no." Swarna got out of her chair and began to pace. "Oh no. Oh, please, no."

"What is it?" Joy asked her. "What's wrong?"

Swarna's chest heaved, and she pressed both hands over her heart. "I've killed him. I've killed Connor."

"What do you mean?" Dr. Dahlman jumped up and grabbed her arm. "What are you talking about?"

"I put penicillin in his IV too."

Chapter Twenty-One

FURIOUS, DR. DAHLMAN PULLED HIS phone out of his pocket. "Get me Dr. Morton!" he barked. "It's urgent!"

Swarna slumped into a chair, a stunned look on her face.

"Is Connor going to die?" Daisy asked in a very small voice.

Veronica went to her and put one arm around her shoulders. "No, he's going to be all right. I'm sure. Dr. Dahlman, you don't have to talk to Dr. Morton. He can take care of Connor without any trouble. You didn't put very much penicillin in that IV, did you, Swarna?"

Swarna shook her head jerkily. "I didn't want to hurt him. Not really. I just didn't want him to leave yet. I didn't know you were going to put more in."

"I didn't put any in."

Swarna gaped at her and then licked her lips. "None?"

"None," Veronica said, her mouth tight. "I would never hurt my son, especially not for some kind of art project I thought would make me famous."

Swarna looked from her to Joy. "She wanted to make me confess."

"Yes," Joy admitted. "It took me a second or two to realize it, and then I thought I'd better let her see if that made the guilty person speak up. When I talked to Camilla, she told me that all of you had an opportunity to tamper with that IV bag. All of you except Veronica."

"I couldn't figure out which one of you three was guilty," Veronica said, "so I thought, actually I hoped, that whoever was doing this to Connor didn't really want him to be hurt. I hoped that, if the situation seemed life threatening, the guilty person would speak up."

"You used a syringe, didn't you?" Joy asked Swarna. "Like you did on those chocolates. Like you learned to do when you were in Africa."

Swarna nodded, not looking at anyone. "I did it when the nurse was distracted with Daisy." She clutched her purse more closely. "The syringe is still in my bag."

Dr. Dahlman held out his hand. "You'd better let me keep that until the police come."

Swarna looked startled for a moment and then handed the bag over to him.

"You were the one who called and said I needed to come get those flowers that had been misdelivered," Daisy told her, her eyes flashing. "And you stole that card Connor was using for a bookmark so you could copy my handwriting and make it look like I was trying to hurt him."

"And then you went to that florist's and had them send Connor flowers you knew he was allergic to," Joy added. "That was after you threw away that letter he got from the college that might be interested in him. Did you have something to do with his knee injury too? Did he really just happen to trip over your camera bag? Or were you trying to add a little drama to that particular scene?"

"I didn't think he'd get more than a few bumps and bruises," Swarna said, her voice barely above a whisper.

"Besides doctoring those candies."

"That peanut oil was risky for him, and for you," Dr. Dahlman said sternly. "You could have misjudged how much you put in the chocolates and had a more severe reaction than you expected. All of this was very foolish of you. And cruel."

"We thought you were our friend," Veronica said, her voice shaking. "You've known Connor since he was a baby. I trusted you."

"I couldn't let him leave," Swarna said, shame and defiance somehow mixed in her expression. "I swear I didn't want to hurt him. I only wanted him to stay and let me finish my film. I've spent fifteen years on it. I couldn't let it be ruined now, just because he didn't want to participate anymore. I was so close."

"Close?" Joy asked her.

"If he had only let me finish, I could have won at all the major film festivals. I know I could."

Dr. Dahlman snorted. "Now filmmakers can win prizes by making documentaries about you."

Rebekah showed up a few minutes later. A short time after that, she and the officer with her read Swarna her rights and escorted her, confiscated purse and all, out of the hospital.

"We'll all have to make formal statements as soon as we can," Joy said afterward, and she sank into a chair, suddenly exhausted. "I'm glad you got her to confess, Veronica. Though I have to admit I was pretty startled when you said you were guilty when you couldn't have been."

"I was the only one I was sure wasn't guilty," Veronica said.

Dr. Dahlman crossed his arms over his chest and looked her up and down. "Humph. That was a pretty convincing little part you played there. Remind me never to get on your bad side."

"That's my boy somebody was messing with," Veronica said with a tearful grin. "I wasn't going to let it keep happening if I could stop it." She turned to Joy. "Thank you so much for caring enough to try to find out what was going on."

"I'm glad this is finally over and Connor will be safe."

"He's doing all right now," Dr. Morton said from the waiting room door.

Veronica ran to him and grabbed both of his hands. "Are you sure? Can I see him?"

"He's sleeping again, but he's fine. I'm afraid he'll have to stay another night, but I'm sure he'll be able to go home tomorrow."

"Oh, thank God." Veronica squeezed his hands. "And thank you, Doctor. Thank you so much."

He gave her an understanding smile. "You go see him. But don't wake him up. He's been through a lot the past few days. But I have to warn you, he's tougher than he seems. I think he'll bounce back from this and be feistier than ever."

She nodded, tearing up again. "All this time I've been trying to raise a child when I really should have realized it was my job to raise a man."

Joy put one arm around her. "I think you've done a fine job."

Veronica hugged her impulsively.

"I hope you don't still think I'd do anything to hurt him," Daisy said, her voice soft and uncertain. "I promise I wouldn't do that to anybody, especially not him."

Veronica took her hand. "I owe you an apology, Daisy. Yes, after those flowers were delivered, I admit I wondered if you could be behind all this, but it really was more than that. I had seen the class notes you had copied for him back then, and after he lost that card he was using for a bookmark, I realized the handwriting was the same. It was very special to him, and I can guess why. I suppose it's something every mother deals with in time."

"It isn't really anything," Daisy said shyly. "He won't even talk to me, so I can't imagine he's actually interested in me. I don't know why he'd keep that card all these months."

"If he didn't like you, he wouldn't have any problem talking to you," Veronica assured her. "Why don't you come sit with me awhile? We can get to know each other a little better while we're waiting for Connor to wake up. Would you like that?"

Daisy nodded rapidly, and the two of them walked across the hall and into Connor's room.

Dr. Dahlman gave Joy a wink. "If Mom's learned to loosen up a little after all this and let her boy start being a man, maybe he won't be so eager to pull up stakes and go to Massachusetts."

"That'll suit you too, won't it?" Joy asked him.

"For now. I think he's still not quite ready to leave home, even if his mother lives nearby. But I also think MIT would be a perfect fit for him, intellectually and temperamentally."

She studied him for a moment. "You're the one who contacted MIT about him, aren't you?"

"I told you you should have talked to his mother about that first, Gene," Dr. Morton said.

"I told them both I didn't think he ought to be in a hurry," Dr. Dahlman said, "but I still think it's good for him to start investigating the prospect. He'll be happier at home if he feels like he can start taking steps toward what he wants to do, even if they're only baby steps." He turned to Joy, one eyebrow raised. "You didn't really think I was behind this, did you?"

"After I heard you and Dr. Morton talking in Dr. Morton's office," Joy admitted, "I had to wonder. You wanted Dr. Morton to keep Connor overnight, and you wanted it to look like that was his idea. And you practically insisted that he give Connor more fluids. That would have been fairly convenient for you, if you had been the one who had planned to keep Connor here."

"I suppose you're right," Dr. Dahlman said. "I only wanted Connor to think the orders came from Dr. Morton so it would seem more like a medical necessity than just my wanting to do more study, but I honestly thought that was best for him, especially the IV. If there was anything self-serving about that request, it was that he would likely not have any of the allergen in his system anymore, and that would give me a cleaner study."

Joy looked at him doubtfully, and then she softened her expression. "I suppose those things have to be taken into consideration."

"True, but that doesn't mean I don't want what's best for the boy. Honestly."

"I hope things calm down now," Dr. Morton said. "I have enough on my plate without this extra side of drama. If we can get Connor through the night and out of the hospital without any more problems, I'll feel like it's Christmas and my birthday all rolled into one."

"Oh." Joy checked her watch and was relieved that she still had plenty of time before she had to get ready for Shirley's party.

"Is everything all right?" Dr. Morton asked her.

"Yes, but I can't lose track of time today. I have a birthday party to go to."

"Ah," the doctor said with a knowing grin. "The famous surprise party."

"You heard about that?"

"Shirley has a lot of friends at the hospital. I've heard the buzz."

Joy hadn't thought to invite him to the party, and they had tried, though evidently unsuccessfully, to limit the guest list to only Shirley's closer hospital friends. Still...

"I think we have room for a couple more if you'd like to come, Dr. Morton. Are you familiar with Hannibal's?"

"Definitely. 'Feeding the soul of the city' as they say. My wife and I love it."

"It's only going to be sandwiches and cake, but you're both welcome. Everybody needs to be there a little before seven, before we get Shirley there. Please come."

"I'll talk to Kelly about it. Thank you."

"Dr. Dahlman—"

"Thank you," Dr. Dahlman said, "but I have to get that conference call rescheduled. I wasn't actually expecting all this to happen right now. If you talk to Veronica, tell her I'll be by to check on Connor as soon as I can." He gave Joy a sly wink. "But don't tell her I'm the one who put MIT in the boy's head."

"All right. I'll keep quiet. I'm going to go check on them right now. Dr. Morton, I hope to see you and your wife tonight."

"Thanks, Joy."

Joy went across the hall and into Connor's room. Daisy and Veronica sat in chairs next to the bed, and it was obvious they had been talking.

"How's he doing?" Joy whispered.

"I'm all right," Connor said, blinking owlishly at her. "But I think I have to get out of here before something else happens to me."

"You're safe," Veronica said, immediately taking his hand. "And nothing's going to happen to you anymore."

She glanced at Joy, obviously wanting her to explain.

"We found out that Swarna was behind everything, trying to keep you here so she could finish her film," Joy told Connor. "I'm sorry."

Connor looked at her and then at his mother and then sank deeper into his pillows. "Man."

That was all he said, but Joy could see the confusion and the feeling of betrayal in his dark eyes. Since before he could really remember, Swarna had been his friend.

"How are you now?" Daisy asked softly, coming into Connor's line of sight for the first time.

He seemed startled to see her there, and then he turned to his mother, but she still had a gentle smile on her face.

"Daisy and I have been talking," she said. "I think we understand each other better now."

"We're only friends," Connor said dismissively.

"Friends are good to have," Veronica told him.

Joy thought that was the best thing she could have said. Whatever might blossom between him and Daisy in the future was up to them.

That evening, Joy told Anne, Evelyn, and Shirley what had happened at the hospital.

"But when I left for the day," Joy said, "Connor was doing really well. Still on an IV, but just fluids again. This time with nothing harmful added."

"Well, I heard that something happened up on two," Shirley said with a shake of her head. "But I sure didn't get any details. That's flat-out crazy."

"Isn't it though?" Evelyn said. "What I heard was that somebody had to chase down the perpetrator and wrestle a penicillin syringe out of her hand. I thought that might be a tiny bit exaggerated, even for hospital gossip."

"I'm glad it's all over," Anne said as she pulled into the parking lot. "And now we can concentrate on the birthday girl."

"Hannibal's!" Shirley said, breaking into a brilliant smile. "I love this place. What a great idea. I was afraid you were going to pick something really, really fancy. Don't get me wrong, I love fancy once in a while. But when I'm with my girls, I like someplace where we can just enjoy ourselves."

"We're going to have fun," Evelyn said.

Joy smiled slyly as she texted Roger to tell him they had arrived. She had left it up to Roger to make sure everything would work from here on out. She pictured what it would be like if things went wrong and felt that sudden heaviness in her stomach, but then she let it go. She didn't have to do everything herself, and Roger was certainly someone she could count on. It was going to be a good night. Perfect or not, they would have fun, and Shirley would know how much everyone loved and appreciated her. That was all that mattered.

"Come this way," Joy said once they were inside with the lively crowd. "We got a private room."

They made their way through the close-set tables, around the guests and staff until they got to the back. With a sly smile at Anne and Evelyn, Joy threw open the door and stepped aside to let Shirley in.

"Surprise!"

Shirley gasped and then laughed at the crowd of people surging toward her. Garrison was the very first.

He folded her in his arms for a moment and then kissed her cheek and presented her with a dozen long-stemmed red roses. "Happy birthday, Shirley."

She squeezed his hand. "Thank you. Thank you all for coming."

More of her friends came up to her, telling her happy birthday, giving her smiles and warm hugs, asking if she had really been surprised, pleased when she assured them she was.

"Oh," she cried, turning after a few minutes to Joy, Evelyn, and Anne. "You got me. I didn't expect anything like this. It's wonderful." She looked around the room, and her eyes filled with tears as she saw her mother sitting at a table with Dot, both of them beaming at her. "You got Mama here too."

"Of course," Anne said. "Without her, we wouldn't have you."

"Surprise, Shirley!" Roger said coming up to them. "Happy birthday!"

"Thank you," Shirley said. "And thank you for coming."

"You'll have to thank Joy. She invited me."

"And Roger arranged for the cake," Joy said. "It was made by a very amazing cake designer."

Joy led them all over to the table where a huge cake was set up. She was sure that somewhere in there was actual chocolate cake, but covering it was a glorious array of flowers of all kinds and colors, a garden of red and pink, yellow, blue, and purple with a variety of green leaves each done in rich-looking icing and all of it surrounding a perfect fondant replica of the hospital's Angel of Mercy.

Shirley stared at it for a silent moment, and then she shook her head. "That's amazing. It's too beautiful to eat. Thank you, Roger. And thank you all too," she told Joy, Evelyn, and Anne.

"We didn't quite know how to decorate it," Evelyn admitted.

Shirley chuckled. "I guess I don't really have a lot of time for hobbies and things like that. Oh, but the flowers are beautiful. And the angel is wonderful."

"We wanted it to be pretty," Anne told her.

"And we wanted it to be like that saying you hear sometimes," Joy added. "'Friends are flowers in the garden of life.' And we're so glad we picked you."

Sudden tears in her eyes, Shirley hugged all three of them at once. "And I'm glad I picked all of you."

Dear Reader,

Do you ever have trouble finding just the right way to celebrate someone's birthday? Sure, it's easy to send a card or buy a cake, but what if the person you want to honor is someone very important to you, someone who needs a truly special celebration? Joy, Evelyn, and Anne really wanted to show Shirley that she is special to them, but they weren't quite sure how. She's not really the type to want expensive gifts or elaborate events.

After worrying about what to do, they finally decided that what she would like best is to spend time with good food, her favorite cake, and her best friends. Material gifts are not usually long-lasting or long remembered, but time spent with loved ones is priceless.

As they say, people won't remember what you said or did, but they will remember how you made them feel. When you give people your precious time, you make them feel special. When you give them yourself, you make them feel loved.

Love,
DeAnna

About the Author

THE AUTHOR OF NUMEROUS TRADITIONALLY published books and with more to come, DeAnna Julie Dodson has always been an avid reader and a lover of storytelling, whether on the page, the screen, or the stage. This, along with her keen interest in history and her Christian faith, shows in her tales of love, forgiveness, and triumph over adversity. A fifth-generation Texan, she makes her home north of Dallas with three spoiled cats and, when not writing, spends her free time quilting, cross-stitching, and watching NHL hockey.

An Armchair Tour of Charleston

Savor the Flavors of Charleston Walking Food Tour

WHAT COULD BE GREATER THAN an afternoon of history, sightseeing, and food?

The Savor the Flavors Walking Food Tour is a great way to see historic Charleston, learn about where the city's traditions came from, and get a sampling of the many cultures that have come together to give the city its unique texture. A nice side benefit is that participants get to sample a variety of Charleston's foods and beverages, giving them ideas about places to try when dining on their own.

On the tour, local professional guides lead adventurers on a two-and-a-half-hour walk to learn about and enjoy the best the city has to offer. The guides describe how South Carolina's food culture has changed over the years, and guests get a feeling for the current scene as they pop into local eateries, bakeries, and popular markets to taste stone-ground grits, pralines, collard greens, South Carolina barbecue, benne wafers, gourmet chocolate, and Southern seafood, a feast for the eyes, ears, minds, and stomachs of Charleston's visitors.

Find out more at:

bulldogtours.com/tours/savor-the-flavors-of-charleston-tour/19

Good for What Ails You

Chocolate Buttercreams

I INCLUDED THESE IN THE book because they're my favorite. I promise I never use them for nefarious purposes.

Ingredients:
Buttercream Filling:

½ cup (1 stick) unsalted butter (must be at room temperature—do not soften in microwave)
4 cups confectioners' sugar
3 tablespoons milk
2 teaspoons vanilla extract
½ teaspoon almond extract
pinch of salt

Chocolate Coating:

4 (4 ounce) bars of semisweet/dark baking chocolate
1 teaspoon vegetable oil

Instructions:

Cream butter and confectioners' sugar together. Add milk, vanilla extract, almond extract, and salt. Cover and chill in refrigerator for no less than an hour.

After mixture has chilled, line a baking sheet with parchment paper. Form filling into tablespoon-size balls and place on parchment paper. Chill for at least another hour.

After filling has chilled for a second time, melt chocolate with the oil and stir until smooth. Let mixture cool for about five minutes.

Drop a buttercream into chocolate mixture, making sure it's liberally coated. Lift it out with fork and then slide it onto parchment-covered baking sheet. Once each buttercream is coated, drizzle remaining chocolate over candies. Add nuts, sprinkles, powdered sugar, or other toppings as desired. Place in refrigerator for about thirty minutes, or until chocolate has set.

Store candies in refrigerator in airtight container for up to two weeks.

Read on for a sneak peek of another exciting book in the Sweet Carolina Mysteries series!

A Hard Pill to Swallow
BY ELIZABETH LUDWIG

OCTOBER DRIFTED LAZILY INTO CHARLESTON. It didn't roar in on a gust of freezing rain or piling snow. There weren't surprising cold fronts to shock the color from the trees. There was merely the slightest dip on the thermometer and the fluttering of the pages on Anne's calendar to mark the seasons. That didn't mean, however, that she couldn't enjoy the creamy spice of pumpkin-flavored coffee on her tongue.

Sighing gratefully, she blinked through the steam rising from her cup to take another careful sip, the Monday morning newspaper rustling between her fingers.

"Anything interesting?" Her husband, Ralph, gave a nod toward the paper then set his own cup on the table next to a heaping plate of bacon and eggs. Lifting one brow, he held out a slice of bacon.

Though it smelled delicious, Anne shook her head. "No, thanks. Already had some." She laid the paper aside and nudged it toward him. "And not to spoil anything for you, but no...there's nothing interesting."

"Mmm." Ralph crunched the bacon and reached for the paper anyway. After swallowing the bite, he said, "I figured the police would have a lead on those muggings by now."

"Me too, or at least I hoped so." She pinched her lips together to stop a troubled sigh. "I just can't get over it. Three attacks, and all of them literally happened right outside the hospital. Wouldn't you think someone saw something?"

Ralph shrugged as he reached for the saltshaker. "Winter is creeping up on us. The sun sets earlier and earlier. By eight o'clock, it's way past dark."

"True." Anne shrugged off the unsettled feeling in her stomach and finished her coffee, then carried her cup to the sink for a quick rinse before placing it in the dishwasher. "Will you start that before you head to the hospital?" She gave a nod toward the cupboard. "Soap is under the sink. I know it's low, but I'll swing by the store after work and pick up more."

"No problem. I'll take care of it."

"Thanks, honey." She pressed a kiss to her husband's cheek, the woodsy scent of his aftershave familiar after forty years of marriage. "Love you."

"Love you too."

Plucking her car keys off a mirrored shelf, Anne shifted her thoughts to Mercy Hospital, where she served as a volunteer and where Ralph ministered as the chaplain. Talk along the halls the last couple of days had centered around the incident that took place three nights ago. A woman from HR had been walking to her car when a shrouded figure appeared from nowhere and knocked her over the head. Fortunately, she was fine, aside from a slight concussion. Still, what the person was after was unclear since the rumor circulating was that nothing had been stolen, just like the first two muggings.

Could they even be called muggings if nothing was taken?

Anne pondered the question as she slid into her parking space at the hospital. Though the sun already peeked over the tallest gable and warmed the red brick walls to a fiery orange, she couldn't help but look over her shoulder as she made her way inside. The idea of someone lurking in the shadows made her nervous. And angry.

"Morning!"

Anne startled at the cheerful voice greeting her from the direction of the gift shop. Joy Atkins's eyebrows lowered in a perplexed frown. "Are you all right?"

Anne shivered and jammed her car keys into the pocket of her smock. "Fine. Got the jitters, is all."

Joy snorted, a sound that only she could make dignified. "You and me both. It's delivery day, so I had to get here early to unlock the back door. I was jumpy as a cricket until the van showed up with my flowers." She came around the counter. "I sure wish they'd figure out who's behind these attacks and what they're after so we could all get back to normal."

Anne grunted her agreement, checked her watch, and then motioned toward the back room of the gift shop, where Joy made coffee to give out to friends. "Do you have a pot on? I've got time for a cup before I need to start stocking inventory."

"Of course I do. I even bought some of that pumpkin spice creamer you like."

Though she'd already had a cup, Anne's mouth watered at the thought of a second helping of her guilty autumn pleasure. "Thanks."

Joy's blue eyes sparkled as she motioned her in. "So it's inventory again today, huh? Aurora still mad at you for skipping out on work and nearly bringing down the entire volunteer organization?"

"Addie was sick, and Lili couldn't get her. Besides, I was only out one day," Anne reached for a cup dangling from a hook behind the coffeepot. On the front it read, COFFEE FIRST...TALK LATER, a fitting sentiment for this particular morning. "But Aurora was really upset, which is strange, because she's not usually like that."

"It's your own fault for being so dependable." Joy's Texas drawl and playful smile softened the teasing. She opened a small fridge under the counter and thumped a bottle of creamer on the counter next to Anne's elbow. "If you were sporadic and untrustworthy, you wouldn't have this trouble."

Anne reached for the creamer. "Okay, okay. I get your point."

"Hmm." Joy snagged a second cup and poured herself some coffee. "So, speaking of the muggings..."

"Were we still talking about that?"

"We are now." She replaced the pot and laced both hands around her cup. "I've been thinking. This last one happened on the south side of the hospital. Do you suppose the mugger hid behind the row of hedges that grows there and that's why no one saw anything?"

Anne fingered the handle on her coffee cup while she thought. "It would be a good spot, I guess. The hedge is tall enough. But wouldn't that mean the mugging was planned and not some random, spur-of-the-moment type thing?" Somehow, the thought made the act all the more menacing. She shook her head and took a hasty sip from her cup. "Anyway, I'm more than happy to leave all that to the police."

"I suppose." Joy's tone said the opposite.

Anne lifted an eyebrow. "The police and security team have everything well in hand. There's no point in the two of us getting involved."

"Make that the three of us." Evelyn Perry joined them in the gift shop and pointed to the coffeepot. "Any more in there?"

Joy moved aside with a wave. "Help yourself."

"Thanks. Is that pumpkin spice?"

Anne nudged the sweetened creamer toward her. "So you heard what I said? And you agree that we're just fine letting the police and security handle things?"

"That's usually best." Evelyn screwed the cap onto the creamer and ambled with her cup to a small table in sight line with the door. Anne and Joy followed. Evelyn took the stirrer out of her cup, licked the end, then laid it on a napkin. "Unless...you know...we actually have a reason to get involved."

"Please don't let that be foreshadowing." Anne shot a glance heavenward. More often than not of late, mysteries like this one tended to get tossed into their laps. "I've got my hands full helping Lili get Addie acclimated to third grade."

Joy scraped a chair out from the table and sat. "Is she still having trouble with her new teacher?"

Anne shrugged. "I'm not so sure it's the teacher. I think Addie just misses her mom. I guess we both thought we'd see Lili more now that she's home from deployment, but those evening classes she's taking really eat up her time and energy. Of course, with our history, I don't dare say too much, even though things are definitely getting better."

Evelyn placed her hand over Anne's, her fingers warmed by the coffee inside her cup. "I'm glad they have you."

Anne smiled at her gratefully. "Thanks."

"You know what you need?" Evelyn crossed to the door and yanked a paper flyer off the glass. "Exercise."

For the span of several seconds, Anne simply stared. Next to her, Joy sat frozen as well, her cup halfway to her mouth. Finally, they looked at each other and broke into laughter.

"I need *what*?" Anne asked, gasping.

"I mean it." Evelyn's gaze bounced between the two of them. Waving the flyer in their faces, she added, "It's a well-known fact that exercise helps relieve stress. And with the hospital offering free fitness classes to staff, it's the perfect opportunity."

"Wait...what?" Anne grabbed the flyer and flipped it over to read. "When did this start?"

"You haven't heard?" Joy set her cup down and tapped the back of the sheet with her finger. "It's a new employee benefit Garrison is trying out to improve morale."

Evelyn nodded. "Exactly. Like I said."

Anne returned her gaze to the flyer. "Yoga, low-impact aerobics, strength and conditioning, CrossFit..." She read the list of instructors and lifted her head. "Basically, a little bit of everything."

"Yep. I was thinking about checking out the low-impact aerobics." Evelyn leaned forward eagerly. "You gals wanna join me?"

Torn with indecision, Anne bit her lip. An exercise class could be fun but... "I'm not sure. We keep Addie pretty late, and by the time we eat and help her with her homework—"

"That's only on Monday, Wednesday, and Friday while Lili's at class. What about Tuesdays and Thursdays?" Evelyn insisted.

"We could even throw in a Saturday morning sometimes," Joy added. Anne's brows rose, and Joy lifted both hands, palms out. "I'm not saying we have to, just that it's a possibility."

"Hmm." Anne thought a moment longer and then agreed with a slow nod. "I guess it wouldn't hurt. It could be a good distraction."

"Speaking of distractions…" Joy angled her head toward the door, where hospital administrator Garrison Baker had just stepped through. "We should thank him for coming up with the idea."

Anne would have agreed, except that Garrison seemed to be making a beeline straight toward them, a frown on his lips and his brow creased with lines of worry.

"There you are," he said. "I was hoping I'd find one of you. Have you heard from Shirley?"

"Shirley?" Anne glanced at her watch. "Is she here? I know she's been taking on some extra shifts, but I didn't think this one started for another hour."

Garrison's eyes rounded and he looked them over, one by one. "You mean…you haven't heard? She didn't call you?"

"About what?" Evelyn demanded. "What's going on?"

Garrison shoved both hands into the pockets of his trousers. "Shirley put in some extra hours on her last shift."

A feeling of foreboding crept over Anne, shooting her pulse into overdrive. "Spill it, Garrison. What are you talking about?"

She didn't think it possible, but the lines on Garrison's brow actually deepened. "It happened last night," he said at last, blowing out a breath. "After she got off work, Shirley was mugged."

A Note from the Editors

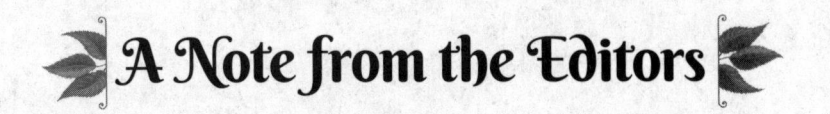

WE HOPE YOU ENJOYED ANOTHER exciting volume in the Sweet Carolina Mysteries series, published by Guideposts. For over seventy-five years, Guideposts, a nonprofit organization, has been driven by a vision of a world filled with hope. We aspire to be the voice of a trusted friend, a friend who makes you feel more hopeful and connected.

By making a purchase from Guideposts, you join our community in touching millions of lives, inspiring them to believe that all things are possible through faith, hope, and prayer. Your continued support allows us to provide uplifting resources to those in need. Whether through our online communities, websites, apps, or publications, we strive to inspire our audiences, bring them together, and comfort, uplift, entertain, and guide them.

To learn more, please go to guideposts.org.

Find more inspiring stories in these best-loved Guideposts fiction series!

Mysteries of Lancaster County
Follow the Classen sisters as they unravel clues and uncover hidden secrets in Mysteries of Lancaster County. As you get to know these women and their friends, you'll see how God brings each of them together for a fresh start in life.

Secrets of Wayfarers Inn
Retired schoolteachers find themselves owners of an old warehouse-turned-inn that is filled with hidden passages, buried secrets, and stunning surprises that will set them on a course to puzzling mysteries from the Underground Railroad.

Tearoom Mysteries Series
Mix one stately Victorian home, a charming lakeside town in Maine, and two adventurous cousins with a passion for tea and hospitality. Add a large scoop of intriguing mystery, and sprinkle generously with faith, family, and friends, and you have the recipe for *Tearoom Mysteries*.

Ordinary Women of the Bible
Richly imagined stories—based on facts from the Bible—have all the plot twists and suspense of a great mystery, while bringing you fascinating insights on what it was like to be a woman living in the ancient world.

To learn more about these books, visit Guideposts.org/Shop